ONE OFF
Not Really an Autobiography

By Barbara Robinson

With Foreword by Maureen Lipman

HUTTON PRESS
1988

Published by the Hutton Press Ltd.
130 Canada Drive, Cherry Burton, Beverley
North Humberside HU17 7SB

Copyright © 1988

No part of this book may be reproduced,
stored in a retrieval system or transmitted in any form,
or by any means electronic, mechanical, photocopying,
recording or otherwise without the prior permission of
the Publisher and the Copyright holders.

Printed and Bound by
Clifford Ward & Co. (Bridlington) Ltd.
55 West Street, Bridlington,
East Yorkshire YO15 3DZ

ISBN 0 907033 75 X

CONTENTS

	Page
Acknowledgements	4
Foreword	5
Part I	
No welcome on the mat	7
The end of the Idyll	22
In no-man's land	33
Back to square one	40
Double life	50
Part II	
Into Africa and beyond	57
An Organ for Wilberforce	65
Israel under fire	70
Joy amid the danger	77
Where 'Chen' means 'Charm'	83
An ambition fulfilled	88
That "Most distressful country"	94
A world beneath our feet	101
"Operation Dhaka"	107
A message of hope	116
The River Project	122
People against poverty	127
The reluctant egotist	131

ACKNOWLEDGEMENTS

I have few acknowledgements to make, for the main theme of this book is, of course, that I have mostly had to fight my own battles!

Credit, where it is due has, I think, been given in the text, but I would also like to thank Charles and Dae Brook of Hutton Press for their unfailing help — and friendship; Maureen Lipman for her Foreword; Hull City Council, and in particular John MacSherrie, for making the Freetown experience possible; and, not least, the staff of William Martins of Savile Street, Hull, for all their advice and assistance in producing my slides and pictures.

Barbara Robinson
November 1988

FOREWORD

Barbara's discoveries in life include someone I'm all too familiar with. Me. As the *Hull Daily Mail's* drama critic, Barbara Duncanson — as she then was — gave me my first "rave". Come to think of it, I've never had a better one. The fact that I was a twelve-year-old schoolgirl when she raved gave her editor cause for concern. He was probably right. On the other hand, it gave my mother cause for jubilation and the purchase of her first scrapbook.

Some of Barbara's more interesting and more durable discoveries are chronicled in the pages of *One Off*, her autobiography. Foremost is her discovery of her own potential, at a rather senior stage in life, after a bleak childhood and an adolescence which was overshadowed by the lonely responsibilities of daughterhood.

Her solace was her work as a journalist and, as "Jane Humber" in the *Hull Daily Mail*, she rejoiced in feeling part of a wider community. In the second half of the book, after the death of her mother, she encourages herself to become part of an even wider community. A worldwide one.

Her book, is full of interesting experiences, brave challenges and poignant thoughts, and I was particularly moved by her sudden awareness of being truly happy for perhaps the first time, whilst walking her dog in the woods, one day after her fifty-fifth birthday.

"Quite simply, for the first time in my adult life, I was appreciating something for its own sake." Before that, "The brighter the moonlight, the more lustrous the stars, the sweeter the scents ... the more I had felt the aching emptiness within." It had taken over fifty years for Barbara to feel young.

A real "one off" and a lovely read.

Maureen Lipman
September 1988

PART I — NO WELCOME ON THE MAT

Life is not what we make it. It is very much a matter of what other people, situations and circumstances make it for us. Shakespeare had it slightly wrong: there's a divinity that rough-hews our ends, shape them how we will — only, of course, if he had written that, the line would not have scanned, nor would it have reflected the sequence of the country craft from which he drew the allusion. No amount of talent, resolve or hard work can in themselves achieve a particular objective. If we gain our goal, it is because a certain element of luck has been on our side. And in no respect is life more of a lottery than in that of human relationships.

This may seem strange to those who have never experienced any difficulty in that direction. To them it must seem that fame and fortune are the illusive elements, and that our own temperament, character and behaviour alone determine whether we are loved, hated or ignored, accepted or rejected, welcomed or shunned.

Not so: a friend who has run a marriage bureau for many years once said, "Finding a marriage partner is a matter of being in the right place at the right time. When I think of all the lovely people who have had to come to me because they could not find anybody themselves, and then look around at all the very ordinary ones who have not had to make the slightest effort, that is the only conclusion I can reach." The same goes for other relationships too, as well as for almost every other aspect of life we can name. Up to a point we have a choice, but that choice is much more limited than most of us realise, or care to admit.

In some respects, my life has been rather like one of those Greek legends which start with dire predictions as to what will happen if a child is born to a particular person or couple. In spite of all precautions, a child *is* born, and at first everything seems to be going fine, as though the Fates have been cheated. But they have not been cheated; they are biding their time, and just when everyone has been lulled into a false sense of security — plop-plop-plop! — they place their darts, or thunderbolts, or whatever symbol you choose, with deadly accuracy.

My parents - brains and beauty, but they knew they were not the right people to have children.

My father and mother, both intelligent, responsible and compassionate people, had the sense to know that they were, nevertheless, not good parent material, and they did not intend to have a family. They suited and complemented each other down to the ground in the beginning, but they were rather like George Bernard Shaw and the actress who is reputed to have said to him, "With your brains and my beauty, think what wonderful children we would have!" To which the scrawny, pock-marked philospher replied, "But what if they should inherit your brains and my beauty?" The only difference was that my mother was as anxious as my father to avoid bringing children into the world.

Father was a brilliant, highly-qualified aeronautical engineer, and I am proud of the fact that he was one of the very "First of the Few", working in the early 1930's on designs for the single-seater fighter aircraft which eventually evolved into the Spitfires and Hurricanes that saved our bacon in the Battle of Britain. Unfortunately, however, he had very poor physical health, and was always nervous and sensitive about his lack of fitness.

Mother was a handsome and charming woman, with personality,

wit and plenty of commonsense, though she was no intellectual. Since childhood, however, she had evidently been dogged by a terrible form of anxiety neurosis, and clearly, if I had inherited my father's bad health and my mother's bad nerves it would have been a disaster.

Small wonder, therefore, that they were devasted rather than delighted to learn that I was in the pipeline. Their fears must have concerned not only the possibility of inherited defects; there was also the question of whether they would be able to cope — or whether either or both of them would be around to cope. My mother later made no bones about the fact that she had gone through all the old wives' remedies for unwanted pregnancy in the book, and it sounded as though she had spent most of the nine months sitting in a hot bath taking gin and liquid paraffin and praying for a miscarriage. I don't blame her one little bit; she did it because she cared deeply about the quality of life. She was not rejecting me — by my reckoning there wasn't a "me" at that stage, and by the time there was, by the time I was a real little human personality in my own right, my parents could not do enough for me.

I had a wonderful childhood — a golden childhood, the memories of which have carried me through all the lonely, frustrating years that were to follow.

This is not going to be a formal autobiography, still less a "memoir". Years will be telescoped into sentences and decades dismissed in paragraphs. I shall certainly not "tell all". But I want to set down sufficient of my history and background to show how it is possible in our society for a completely extrovert person to spend most of his or her life locked into a social vacuum from which there seems to be no escape. This may ring a few bells with readers who have found themselves in similar situations, and may even bring some comfort to those who may have felt that their case was unique. Then I want to show how I have tried to play the hand that was dealt to me, especially in the past five years, during which I was at least able to make a few exciting and worth-while things happen, even if they were not the things I originally set out to achieve.

I know little of my family history, especially on my mother's side, and to attempt to record any of it would involve so much guesswork, so much reading between lines and swallowing of pinches of salt that I have decided to let those sleeping dogs lie and begin my story at the point where my mother had her worst fears confirmed by the doctor.

The next day, she once told me, she met her sister-in-law and blurted out, "Oh Cissie, something terrible's happened — I'm going to have a baby!" My aunt Cissie — her name was Elizabeth, but, like many female siblings of the time she was called by that popular diminutive for "sister" — registered astonishment. "But Peggy, that's wonderful!" she replied. "I do envy you..." After that, Mother realised that it was not the done thing for an eight-years-married woman with a professional working husband to register dismay at becoming pregnant, so from then on she and Father tried to put a good face on it.

The reasons for their voluntary childlessness cannot have been obvious even to their closest friends and members of the family, who were all delighted for them. Father was a fine-looking man, tall, dark and always well, if conservatively, dressed, and he was probably anxious not to let it be widely known, especially by prospective or current employers, that he suffered from physical weaknesses. He had been an outstanding student, being awarded the coveted Whitworth Memorial Medal at the Imperial College of Science, and everyone, including his one-time tutor (who later became his brother-in-law) predicted that he would have a highly successful career. It was not to be, however. Again, even allowing for the recessions and depressions of the 1920's and 30's, which badly affected the aircraft industry until Churchill's prophetic warnings began to be heeded, the main problem appeared to be that poor Father was never in the right place at the right time. He never got the right job and always seemed to feel that his brains were being picked and his knowledge exploited by people without a quarter of his qualifications. If he had been more fortunate, it is possible, I believe, that he could have found the time — and, of course, the money — to have some surgical repair work done, which might have made a lot of difference to his general wellbeing, but he never got around to it.

Mother's trouble was in that embarrassing grey area between the mental and the physical, and naturally she tried to hide, or "rationalise" it. Basically, I am convinced, it was physical — some kind of biochemical malfunction, possibly connected with the thyroid or with the adrenalin secretions — but it was never diagnosed, as she could never be persuaded to see a specialist. In many ways, she was like any one of a dozen show-business stars one could name. They brought laughter and pleasure to thousands, though they themselves were tormented by neuroses, and their personal lives were a mess. Mother neither rose to those heights or sank to those depths, but the pattern of her life was similar, and I now strongly suspect that her early and complete break with her own large Suffolk family and her lack of any long-standing close friendships was due to the fact that although she was "lovely to look at, delightful to know" — superficially, at any rate — when her nerves were at her, as the Irish so tellingly put it, she could be hell to live with.

When she met Father, however, she must have had the wretched thing more or less under control. He was by all accounts a nervous and lonely young man, forced by his work to live away from home, and she was just what he needed. Vivacious in a ladylike kind of way, intelligent but not intellectual, sophisticated rather than cultured, she made him laugh, taught him how to relax, brought some fun into his life. To the end, he adored her. She introduced him to light musical shows and the classic Music Hall, which he grew to love. I like to think that in their courting days in World War I they were rather like King George VI and Queen Elizabeth in World War II. When, after a harrowing day visiting bomb-sites and hearing bad news, the King returned weary and depressed to the private apartments in the Palace, the Queen, we are told, would say, "Come, Bertie - let's go and see the Crazy Gang!" The equerry would discreetly make the arrangements and the royal couple would slip into the theatre to escape for a couple of hours into the healing world of comedy. Alas, while our delightful "Queen Mum" was also able to put on her tiara and support the King with charm and grace on State occasions, my poor Mum was not, when it came to it, able to adapt to the role of a rising professional man's wife. And my coming did not help, bringing an extra responsibility they had not bargained for and straining the delicate mental balance on both sides.

My actual birth, however, seems to have been, in truth, quite a happy event. In Uxbridge, on a fine June night, I slipped quickly and easily into the world, a tiny, slimy baby turning the scales at just over five pounds. Even Mother, with her genius for making heavy weather of things, could not complain that she had had a bad confinement. Despite the fact that she had insisted well in advance that a large supply of chloroform should be on hand — "enough for an elephant", the doctor said — she hardly needed it, and apparently joked with the staff throughout the delivery. Like many neurosis sufferers, she could sometimes sail through an ordeal which would have upset a normal person. Such people, I have discovered, are neither more nor less brave than other people; they simply have a cock-eyed sense of fear.

Within days, however, it must have been obvious that something was wrong, and my guess is that severe post-natal depression had set in, for there was nothing physically wrong with either of us. At all events, Mother was kept in the little cottage maternity unit for a month — a long stay even in those days of more protracted confinements — and even then the staff made some excuse to offer to keep the baby a bit longer, probably giving Mother a chance to get home and readjust. However, she no doubt felt that to go home minus baby after all that time would look suspicious to friends and in-laws, so she declined the offer.

Luckily, there was a sensible, down-to-earth woman living next door. Mrs Moore had raised half-a-dozen kids of her own and loved having babies around. I suspect that, with Father's collusion and maybe a pound or two slipped over the fence, she virtually acted as an unofficial nanny for the first few months, and, in fact, my very first memory is of her pink face, grey bun and white bib-overall as she leaned over my pram with a bunch of scarlet sweetpeas in her hand.

Neither of my parents was religious, but I was duly christened in the local parish church — mainly, I guess, to please Mrs Moore, who officiated as godmother. Dear Mrs Moore! I wonder what became of her? After we moved away, I believe my parents kept in touch with the family for a while, but contact was eventually lost.

I must have been about 18 months old when we left the Uxbridge area for Cheltenham. Father had given up his job with Fairey Aviation, being dissatisfied with his conditions, and had taken a position with the Gloucester Aircraft Company.

Again, I do not think it proved to be exactly what he wanted, but, with a child to support and the time ticking away — he was now nearing 40 — he settled down and made the best of it, working at home on his own designs, mainly at weekends.

At first we lived in a flat, and here again my mother was lucky, for the basement was tenanted by a nice old couple who served as caretakers. By now, I was quite a fetching toddler, and they were happy for me to spend a good bit of time with them, which relieved the pressure on her. I do remember summer afternoons with Mother in the park, however, where a green bank, thick with daisies, and a pair of black swans, created one of those images which, as the poem says, is " — such a little thing, to remember for years, to remember with tears."

Father's position with the company must have been reasonably good, despite his grumbles, because when I was about three we moved into a house in a Cotswold village. The house itself was a bad joke; it might have been designed by Heath Robinson with a little help from Emmett, and although it had mains water and a flush toilet — when it worked — there was no gas or electricity. It was not the price alone which persuaded my always-impecunious parents to take it, however; the setting was perfect, amid hills and woods and meadows and old farmhouses and cottages, besides which a large garden, orchards and a paddock went with the house.

What did it matter that the hot-water system for the bath consisted of an ancient, evil, asthmatic geyser that emitted nothing but a thin stream of rusty brown water when meth-primed and lit? The nightingales sang in the white and purple lilac trees all the sweet summer long. What did it matter that the flush toilet frequently went wrong and the septic tank got a bit whiffy in hot weather? The old wooden privy, smothered in rambler roses, which had been there long before the new-fangled loo was installed, was recalled to use. What did it matter that the house was a longish walk from the railway station, up a muddy lane? The lawn was a galaxy of daisies, the garden a sunburst of daffodils in spring, the spreading bed of lily-of-the-valley in the shady elbow of the wall more than cancelled out the septic tank, great bunches of mistletoe grew on the gnarled apple-boughs, and there was a swaying wych-hazel tree standing sentinel at the gate — I was convinced that a witch really lived in it!

By now it was becoming apparent that my parents' fears of genetic disaster were unfounded. I had not inherited anything significant from either of them, and the strenuous efforts to dislodge the foetus that eventually became me had done no damage either. My father's brains had certainly not been passed on; he was a mathematical prodigy while I could not add two and two, but his bad health had not been transmitted either; I was a disgustingly fit little beast, give or take the usual childhood upsets. I had not inherited my mother's good looks or attractive personality — we were absolute

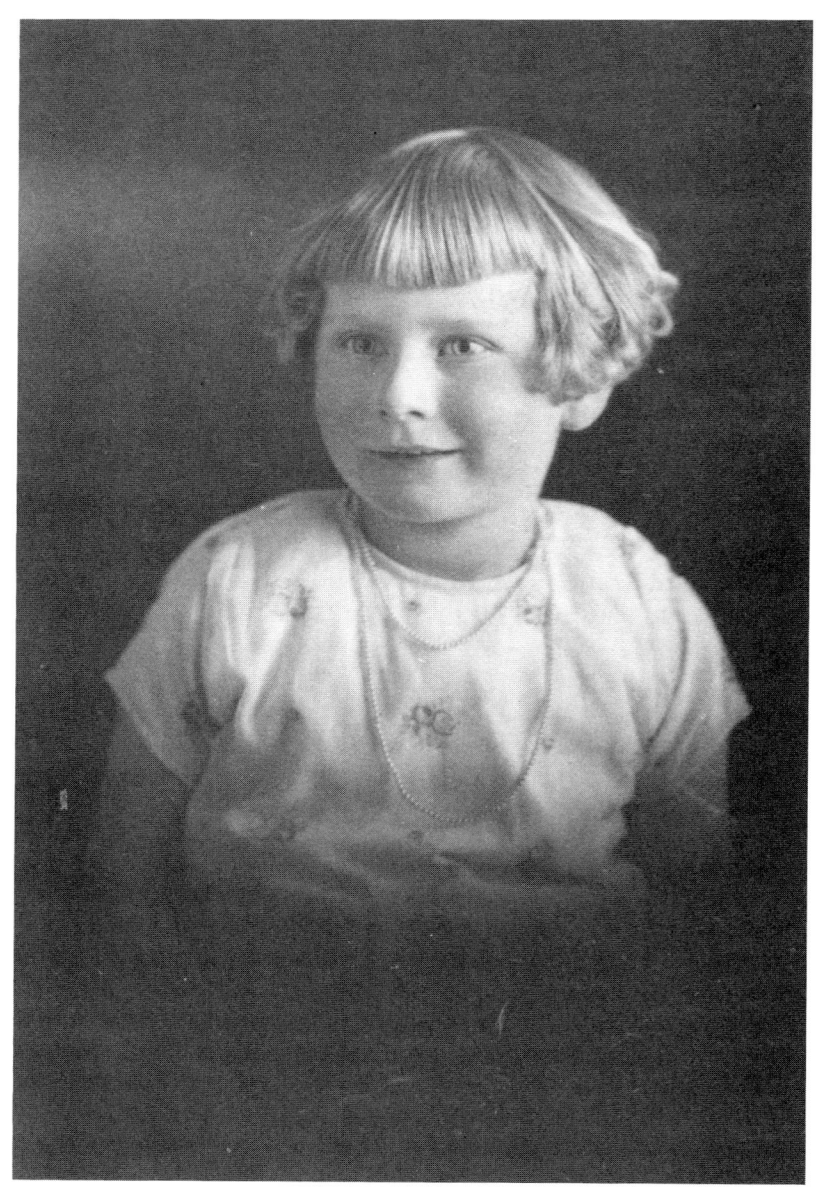

The golden years begin.

chalk and cheese. But, mercifully, neither had I picked up her neurotic traits. Despite all the stress I have since been through, I have never quite gone over the edge into a breakdown — though it has been a near thing sometimes — nor have I had recourse to psychiatry.

As we were settling into the house, a miracle had been taking place. My mother was moving into a long, blissful period of remission, and this heralded our golden age. Why — how — it happened I don't know. It may have been a natural phenomenon, or she may, indeed, have felt more happy and secure, though I have always believed that body-chemistry, and not circumstances, was the key to her condition, and that it was the neurosis that created the traumas and rejections, not the other way round. It was not until many years later that I recalled that her improved outlook at that time coincided, oddly enough, with a goitre which she developed shortly after we arrived in Cheltenham.

Although she would never consult a doctor about her hang-ups, she was not so reluctant to seek advice on some visible complaint, as she did when the swelling appeared in her throat. According to the conversations I overheard on her return the doctor had laughed — he had seen it all before. Cheltenham, it seemed, had a low iodine count, and was nearly as bad as Derbyshire for incidence of goitre. He prescribed some small tablets and also told her to massage the swelling with some greeny-brown iodine ointment. It may have been coincidence, but all the while she was taking those tablets she appeared to be as near normal as made no difference, and when she stopped taking them, her nerves began plaguing her — and us — again. Of course, no-one suspected that there might be a possible connection, as the treatment was not supposed to have anything to do with nerves, but if someone had only put two and two together it might have been worth pursuing the thyroid angle to see if it worked.

In our weirdly-constructed home she made jam and pickles and home-made wine, and cooked splendid meals on a battery of oil-stoves supplemented by an old-fashioned kitchen range. She was quite reasonably sociable and hospitable, exchanging visits with the in-laws, with Father's colleagues and their families, and with neighbours, and even taking part in some village events — though she drew the line at joining the Women's Institute!

She was a splendid mother, too, organising treats and trips and

We had a maid, Gladys, who became one of the family.

holidays and little, unexpected presents in addition to the customary cornucopias of Christmas and birthday gifts — I was lucky in that my birthday came almost exactly half-way between one Christmas and the next. Perhaps she tended to panic, but then, so did most of the mothers I knew.

For a time we had a little live-in maid, Gladys, who became part of the household and accompanied us on picnics in the woods and fields during the seemingly endless summers.

One day, a big, red fox broke cover and streaked past us, pursued by our fat mongrel, which quickly gave up the chase. I remember, too, the haymakers in the fields, seeing men using scythes in long, rhythmic sweeps and others raking the fallen grasses into rows where we children played and tumbled. I can still smell the sweet, sharp scent of the hay. I recall gathering cowslips in the springtime and seeing the embankments thick with violets and primroses as our little train puffed by, picking blackberries in the autumn, collecting big, shiny conkers, from beneath the horse-chestnut trees and seeing a pony plodding round an old-fashioned cider press as the red and russet apples tumbled into the crusher. I recall the strange, white shape sculpted by the snow in the lanes and gardens in winter, the brilliant sunsets I tried to capture with my paints and crayons — and quite successfully, too, in my own opinion: if God wanted any help, he had only to ask!

Then there were the old farmhouses and cottages, some whose only water supply was a pump in the yard, but whose interiors were a magic evocation of frozen Victoriana, for they had not changed in the long married lifetimes of their occupants. They were still a jumble of family photographs and portraits and sentimental prints of children and angels. There were wicker chairs, horsehair sofas that prickled the bare legs of a lightly-clad child of the 1920's, antimacassars and fringed chenille tablecloths in red or green. Along the mantelpieces were ranged Staffordshire dogs and figurines, tinkling chimes that sent prisms of light dancing round the room on a sunny day, and clocks that reminded me of the one in *"Alice Through the Looking Glass"* that my grandmother sent me on my fourth birthday.

Foldyards were often a squelch of midden, but it was delicious to feel the rough tongues of the baby calves sucking our fingers, or to see the hens squawking and fluttering as they fought for the grain we threw to them - no factory farming in those days! To this day, I cannot get hysterical over dog-droppings. In my countryside environment there seemed to be ordure everywhere, and we accepted it as a part of Nature — a very important part, since, in its appropriate forms, it was collected and used as fertiliser. Every home in the village had a big scraper by the door, usually fitted with brushes at either side, and we children were conditioned as soon as we could walk to use it to remove mud and other matter from our little boots and wellies, which were then taken off as we entered the house and replaced by slippers or house-shoes kept in the porch or close to the door. I cannot remember any really bad accident with animal muck — but I can remember laughing myself into a state of breathlessness and wet knickers at the antics of kittens playing with a ball of wool.

I had a long and happy pre-school life, and if every child had as good an environment as I had in those days, I could wish nothing better for any of them. I think we send our children to school too soo, for many can do little but play in their first year, which wastes the time of trained teachers. By the time I started, at nearly seven, I was ready and eager to learn, and had a fair idea of what school was all about.

The reason I was kept at home for so long was purely practical. The nearest private school was a train-ride away in Cheltenham, and I was considered too young to manage it on my own. There was nothing wrong with the village school from an educational point of view; the teachers were splendid, dedicated people, and I suspect now that some of them were gentlewomen with private incomes who did their work as a social service, ploughing their wretched salaries back into treats for the children and aid for the poor families. But one would have had to be a fanatical Socialist to send one's child to such a school if one could afford anything better.

It was not just a question of accents or rough habits, nor of head-lice or "us little purple heads with ring-worm", as Lancashire comedian Tony Capstick put it in his powerful monologue on the social scene of the '30's — though I do remember seeing children with part-shaved heads painted with the tell-tale gentian violet. Much more serious ills were rife in those days — scarlet fever, diptheria and even tuberculosis, including the cruel bovine variety that came from infected milk and resulted in wasted and crippled limbs. Although better-off families were not immune, the risks were far greater among the poor.

I dimly remember the schools inspector knocking on the door one day, and my mother, in her poshest accent, reassuring him that the matter was in hand, that my father was "a Bachelor of Science", and that they were teaching me themselves. That was not strictly true; I was never given formal lessons at home. But I was stimulated in every way — talked to, read to, played with, taken on visits and to theatres, cinemas and concert-parties and encouraged to listen to "the wireless" and to take part in adult conversation. This, I am convinced, is the finest form of pre-school education, far better than crashing about in a church hall with a dozen other kids in a miasma of noise that makes articulate conversation impossible...but not all children are as lucky as I was.

At that period, I was getting the best of both worlds. From Father and his people were coming all the educational impulses — the good books, the visits to museums and art galleries, the interesting people coming and going. Daddy, bless him, even tried to teach me the rudiments of mathematics and science, though my failure to grasp them proves to my own satisfaction, if to nobody else's, that the notion that feminine lack of interest in these subjects is due to biased conditioning, is a load of rubbish. From Mother came all the lovely little, silly fun-things — the icecream and the donkey-rides at the seaside, the surprise presents, the Tin Pan Alley music. Later, I was to develop a love of the classics, but, while Bach belongs to the ages, and I like Bach just fine, I am glad that we had Jack Payne and his band on the old wind-up gramophone when I was a child, for that relates to my own generation alone, and it gives me a warm sense of belonging in a particular time and place in human history.

The only extended family of which I was aware in those days consisted of my grandmother, three uncles (including the one who had been Father's tutor), three aunts and a growing number of cousins, which eventually reached a total of 10. Most were settled in the London area, and one group were in India, doing what, to my fury, it is often now said that "we never did" in our days of Empire: teaching the highest of technology to the Indians and working with them in mutual affection and respect. We did not see much of our people but there was a continuity of contact which was sufficient to give me a feeling of being part of a family. There always seemed to be a letter in the post, a little gift coming, or a visit being planned, even if it was six months or more away.

There is always a price to be paid for every blessing in this world, and despite what I have said about the benefits of a long and happy pre-school life, it did exact a toll. I clearly cannot have had sufficient contact with other youngsters of my own age. At the time I was not aware of this; I was blissfully happy in my little world of caring adults, but it was to lead to a certain difficulty in making peer relationships. One of Father's colleagues lived nearby with his wife and two children, a boy and girl slightly older than I, and I had a fair amount of contact with them, including participation in memorable Christmas and birthday parties, Bonfire Nights and other celebrations. After a while, too, a widow from Lancashire moved into the cottage next door to us with two grown-up sons and a small daughter, Dorothy, who became my closest friend. But evidently it was not quite enough.

All things considered, I took to school life very well, quickly caught up with the class, then shot ahead to somewhere near the top. At first, I related quite well to my fellow pupils, but after a while it became obvious that I was too adult-orientated — a teacher's pet and a bit of a swot. I basked in the approval of the grown-ups and hated being in trouble. Much play, I discovered, consisted of breaking the rules and seeing how far one could get away with it. Bad behaviour carried a good deal of status among one's peers and vice-versa, and not wanting to go along with this, I became rather unpopular. Understandably, I ran into some rather nasty teasing — bullying is too strong a word — and for a time I "went off" school altogether.

It was not that I was a particularly nice child. I had many faults, some of them more unpleasant than ordinary naughtiness. I could, of course, be noisy and silly and self-willed. I could whinge with the best, and must have seemed maddeningly precocious at times. I particularly disliked being patronised, and would sulk thunderously if offended. Much of the time, I reckoned, I was being expected to behave in a grown-up way, accompanying the adults to restaurants and places of entertainment, or on social visits, all of which I enjoyed very much. But in return for my on-the-whole good behaviour I expected to be treated as an adult, and if reproved or scolded I was apt to take it badly.

How did my parents view me in those days? With Father more-or-less reconciled to his bread-and-butter job and working on his own designs at home, and Mother so much better, they really seemed to like having me around. They must have felt that, after all, things had turned out for the best. Having a child must, I think, have given my mother a certain status, both in the social circle in which she was expected to move and with the family. She had never got on with her mother-in-law and was wary, too, of the others, fearing, perhaps, that despite her looks and charm, she must have seemed to them a "girl out of nowhere". Now, by producing a daughter, she had at least fulfilled her maternal function, particularly in the eyes of my grandmother, who was Italian and placed high priority on motherhood. At all events, relationships at this time seemed cordial enough.

Growing up in sunshine and sea air.

THE END OF THE IDYLL

When I was eight years old, things began to go wrong. The Fates were priming their thunderbolts. Father was made redundant, along with a number of others. He was allowed to stay on for a time at a reduced salary, in order to seek another post, but it was a big shock and a bitter blow.

Just when he could have done with a companion who was utterly strong and supportive, Mother's old trouble started to creep back. Truth to tell, I am not sure just when this set in, as up to then there had been plenty of other people around and I had not been so sensitively aware of her personality changes. She may not have been so consistently stable as I had imagined, and it is possible that some diplomatic manoeuvring may have had to be done to cushion me against the fact that from time to time she was "not quite herself". Now, however, there was no mistaking that something was amiss. She repeatedly went down with distressing bouts of what I can, again, only surmise was triggered by some form of manic-depression, and even between times she was struggling to disguise irrational fears which, in particular, affected our social life.

She still loved a visit to the Music Hall or cinema, or an outing of some kind involving just the three of us, but she began to dread any kind of organised or pre-arranged activity. The giving or receiving of hospitality became an ordeal; she wanted neither to visit nor to be visited. She could not bear to be asked to do anything, and the simplest request made her nervy and irritable. If she was so much as asked to make a cup of tea over and above what she had planned to do that day, it was as though her glands sent up enough extra adrenalin to cover running away from an earthquake, and the excess, racing around the system with no fight or flight to burn it up, caused intense, even physical distress, requiring a shot of "Dutch courage" to calm her down.

If only she had said to Father at that stage: "Frank, I'm terribly sorry - just when we could have done without it, this has had to happen -" and together they had tried to work out a solution, things might have turned out very differently. But anxiety neurosis does not work that way; victims seem to feel so ashamed and inferior because of their strange, intangible, invisible sickness that they just cannot live with it — especially since, deep down, they often seem convinced that they are really very special people with special powers, destined for great things.

So, instead of expressing concern and trying to compensate, as most physically ill people seem to be able to do without any loss of dignity or self-esteem, they become arrogant and fault-finding, as though to divert attention from their own condition. They become past-masters at "rationalising" their hang-ups with a battery of unanswerable excuses, and they nearly always find a convenient scapegoat or two on which to dump the blame. Perhaps this is all part of a self-protective mechanism without which the alternatives might be suicide or insanity?

Father, sensitive and self-critical by nature, and now demoralised by unemployment, was too easily persuaded that it was all his fault, or was, at any rate, due to the worry engendered by the situation. He must also have wondered whether he had been wise to make the switch from his previous job.

It seemed as though he was out of work for a long time, but it cannot really have been more than a few months. Fortunately, he had patented a couple of his own designs, including an ingeniously modified monoplane wing, and he managed to interest the Blackburn company in this project. They agreed to take him on the staff and to develop a prototype. Father went up to Yorkshire to get things moving and Mother and I remained in Gloucestershire until the house was sold — no easy matter in view of its lack of amenities. Later, Mother used to say that Father was none too pleased when we finally joined him — "he was wrapped up in his work and didn't want us." But I can now see that if this was in any way true, there was a certain amount of excuse for it. It must have been a relief to get away from us at that stage and to be able to devote himself undisturbed to the work he loved. The job was not highly paid, but it must have been something he had always wanted, and, after all, the company were spending quite a lot on the development.

Personally, I could not wait to get to the new home and make a fresh start. This was the time when I had run into a spot of trouble at school, and I longed to get away. I mugged up all that an eight-year-old could about the place to which I was going, and was in a rare state of excitement and anticipation when the furniture van came and we got into the car to make our way northwards.

For the first six months, while my parents were house-hunting, we lodged with a very nice family in Brough, and I was enrolled at a small private school nearby. This was supposed to be a temporary arrangement, but in fact I was to spend the rest of my school life there.

We walked into instant friendship. The aircraft industry was in those days a closely-knit society, much as the space industry must be today, one supposes, and Father's colleagues and their wives made us very welcome. We were invited out to tea almost every day and the women did their best to orientate my mother into the scene, advising her where the best shops were to be found, describing the theatres, restaurants and places of interest, and recommending a doctor, a dentist who was "good with children", a music teacher who "got them on very well" and so on. I was invited to join the local dance class and the riding school. I had made a start with ballet lessons in Cheltenham, when my mother had made me the most beautiful little dance dress of blue crepe-de-chine trimmed with rosebuds, which I thought was the prettiest in the class. I longed to begin learning to ride; during my first term at school I would draw nothing but horses in the freestyle session.

The friendly reception and long rest from household cares should have set Mother up nicely, but, as I remember, she was still edgy and complaining, so after the summer holidays the search for a suitable house intensified, and they bought a very nice "semi" in what I later discovered was considered the most prestigious part of the area. Some new furniture was bought to supplement what was sent up from the store, and we moved in.

Still things were not right. Mother resented the long and irregular hours Father had to spend at the works, and did not really approve of his poring over drawing-board and slide-rule at home. When his wing was actually fitted to a plane, which then took off with Daddy aboard, she greeted his triumphal announcement with fury: "You're not insured for flying!" she stormed. "What's going to become of us if anything happens to you?"

Desperately insecure, she hated to see money being spent on anything but essentials. Worst of all, she found it impossibly irksome to go along with the social round, which was, of course, a vital factor for Father at that crucial stage of his career, and which ought to have been very pleasant and fulfilling for her too. A normal woman could not have waited to show off her lovely new home, or to return some of the friendly hospitality we had received while we were living in lodgings, but she kept putting it off, fobbing off my pleas for a party and giving Father a hard time whenever he invited anyone home for a meal or an overnight stay. In fact, it reached a stage when the poor man could do nothing right.

A year ended, another started. At the works there were the inevitable tensions as the prototype was tested to its limits, and the equally inevitable personality clashes. Eventually it all proved too much. Father had a complete breakdown, and after some harrowing weeks he was admitted to a private clinic in York. On reflection, it was probably yet one more classic case of the wrong person ending up in hospital!

Father was there for three months, and would no doubt have stayed longer, but it was very expensive, and as a preparation for discharge, he was one day taking part in an outing with other patients when he slipped off the kerb into the path of a bus in one of York's narrow streets...

Our little Scots doctor was a solid source of comfort, and relatives quickly arrived to deal with the crisis. After the funeral, which I did not attend, I was parked at a farmhouse where my teacher also lived, while the in-laws took Mother home with them to recuperate and to discuss the future. It was then that a disagreement arose which virtually cut me off from all extended family relationships.

What apparently happened was this: in a haze of "medicinal" brandy and sedatives, Mother could only keep repeating what was uppermost in her mind: What was she going to do for money? How was she going to manage? Would the insurance company pay out? This shock reaction that the breadwinner has selfishly "upped and died" is by no means uncommon in such cases, I believe, and in no way reflects the true emotions of the widow, but, not unnaturally, the family were deeply hurt. Father had been the brightest star in an all-round clever brood, and although they acknowledged that he was not without his faults, they loved him very much. The old suspicions about Mother's strange lack of background must have been re-activated, and maybe they suspected that her instability might have contributed to the events leading up to the tragedy. I don't know; I wasn't there. I was, strange to say, quite enjoying my stay at the farm.

I look back on this with regret, for Daddy had been good to me.

But the rows of recent years, which Mother always won, and the terrible deterioration in his condition had left a biased impression in my eleven-year-old mind. Daddy was the sick, nervy, difficult, useless one; Mummy was the sane, sensible, practical one who got everything done. If one of them had to go, thank goodness it was Daddy and not Mummy. When all this was sorted out, Mummy and I would be much better on our own.

Mother returned to the North, I came back from the farm and we went home. The links with the in-laws were not completely broken, for a somewhat desultry correspondence was kept up, mainly to keep tabs on my welfare, I suppose, but to all intents and purposes I had, in a matter of a few weeks, lost not only a father but a whole family.

The financial situation was dire, though years later I realised that it ought not to have been all that bad. Although her income had stopped, my mother's capital assets, thanks to the "Prudential", were quite good, including, as they did, the house, freed from all mortgage debt. A reasonably resourceful widow of forty-seven could have used these assets in any one of a number of different ways to create quite a good living, besides giving herself a chance to rebuild her life and make new friends. Also, Mother had contacts, if not in high places, at least in responsible middle-class circles.

But she must have realised that, in her condition, if she went to anyone for help they would only give her advice she could not take. And when they discovered why — when they found out about the horrible bouts of personality disorder and the neurotic fears which made it so difficult for her to live a normal life at the best of times — they would undoubtedly have put great pressure on her to take treatment. That she was not prepared to face. I think she was convinced that there was no cure, and that all that would happen if she submitted to psychiatry was that she would be put through a useless, humiliating ordeal and be no better at the end of it. In the process, she might well have lost me. So she preferred to sit tight and pretend that there was nothing wrong with her that she could not cope with in her own way. She preferred poverty and social isolation to the alternatives.

Sometimes, too, in cases such as hers, it takes more courage to give in than to soldier on, more guts to make a decision to go to someone and say, "I can't cope — please take over", than to keep one's head down and take one day at a time, hoping that it will all come right in the end.

She always maintained that doctors who had been consulted in her youth had advocated using homely, pragmatic remedies from the sideboard cupboard rather than specialist help. Allowing for the fact that we all tend to accept the advice we want to accept and forget, or bend to our own interpretation, that which does not please us, this may well have been true, and if it was, reasons are not hard to imagine. At that time, round about the turn of the century, mental hospitals must have been terrible places, and any GP worth his salt would try to keep a patient out of one, especially a young girl from a good family. Besides, a doctor of that era had the whole family to think about. There was a great deal of fear concerning anything that smacked of mental disorder, and if it was known that a girl was under treatment, even as an out-patient, it could affect her sister's marriage chances or her brother's job prospects.

In some ways, it might have been better if my mother's trouble had been just a little worse. If some real crisis had built up and she had been taken into hospital so that the whole thing had come out into the open, the resulting intervention might have been beneficial to both of us. As it was, she always pulled back from the brink before things went that far. The result was that the beastly thing played cat-and-mouse with us for the next forty-two years.

We continued to live in the same house, which was a strange decision in itself, as the place needed a company director's salary to maintain it properly, and there was no way she could make it work for her. Over the next few years we had the odd boarder staying with us, some for quite long periods, but while this might have been a useful way of topping up a reasonable income, it did not begin to meet all our needs. In the end, Mother had to take out a mortgage on the house, and, with stringent economies, this tided us over until I was old enough to sort things out.

Meantime, I continued to attend the same little school. It was run by a remarkable woman, Miss Mildred Suddaby, an Oxford graduate who had once been a lecturer in a teacher training college, but had later opted to run her own small school and supplement her income by coaching older students in the evenings and vacations. When I was about twelve, and it was clear that my mother was too paralysed with nerves and worry to take any initiative concerning my education, Miss Suddaby volunteered to keep me on and put me through a kind of matric-type examination which, if I gained the right grades, could set me on course for anything up to university level.

This was agreed, and before I was fifteen, I had pretty well gone through the syllabus. Miss Suddaby suggested that another term might clinch the grades, and as the very modest fees — in fact, they were quite ridiculously low — were virtually being paid through little gifts sent discreetly, a bit at a time, by the family in London, I was able to stay on, taking the old tough Oxford School Certificate in eight subjects with four credits and four distinctions.

How I did it I don't know, for, with no adult confidante to talk to, my mother was constantly pouring out all her troubles to me, often keeping me awake at night when her anxiety was at its height, and inevitably transmitting some of it to me.

My little bit of scholastic success, such as it was, can be attributed almost entirely to sheer good teaching. Using a rented Sunday School room in a Congregational chapel, a collection of old books and a few bits and pieces of equipment, that incredible woman taught me the nature and history of the universe, no less. She had no laboratory, but I gained credit passes in botany, chemistry and physics. She had no art equipment, but I got a credit in art. It all goes to show that chalk and talk does work, when it is well done.

The fact that I had no out-of-school activities — the ballet and riding had, of course, stopped with our income — no doubt concentrated the mind wonderfully too. And credit must also go to the old steam radio in the days of Lord Reith, when talks, classic plays, and programmes such as the *Brains Trust* provided invaluable educational back-up.

At my first school, it had been discovered that although I was pretty average at most things and abysmal at maths, I had a very good aural memory. When I had been at school for only a few weeks, the teacher asked our little beginners' class whether any of us could sing any of the songs from the school show, then in rehearsal. I needed no second bidding; at the age of two I would stand on a table and sing a saucy old Marie Lloyd song to entertain a roomful of people, so this was a piece of cake. I went through the whole of the first scene, cue-lines, lyrics and all. I didn't think I had done anything clever, but at an Open Day shortly afterwards, the teacher told my parents that she had been astonished (and, I suspect, a little embarrassed) by my performance!

Miss Mildred Suddaby. This incredible woman taught me the nature and history of the Universe - no less.

Most school work, apart from maths, I actually liked. I would voluntarily learn whole Shakespeare plays and all the great lyric poems of Shelley, Keats and the other Romantics. It was hard to say where homework ended and pleasure-reading began — though I was not immune to the lure of school stories and cheap adventure paperbacks, which I shared with the girl next door, one of my very few neighbourhood friends.

When we had a boarder, he was kept very much in his own part of the house, and took his meals alone. Mother, who was a superb cook, slipped in shyly with the food and kept conversation to a minimum. But one of our guests played the piano well, and in this way I got to know many of the popular classics, for his repertoire was large, ranging from Bach, Beethoven and Mozart to Debussy. This, I think, was the start of my appreciation of music.

Mother hated being a "landlady" — another strange thing, for most widows, especially those who have never worked outside the home, tend to like having a "man about the house" again — someone to cook for, to mend for, to talk to, or even to make burglars think twice about breaking in! But for us, of course, it was a constant strain, a constant battle for control, or for ways of covering up when that control gave way. During the war, she kept the spare rooms occupied only because she feared that otherwise she might have military personnel or evacuees billeted on her.

It was a bizarre situation. There we were, living in that lovely house in a leafy, stockbroker village, yet we hadn't two halfpennies to rub together. I was receiving virtually the same kind of education as the future Queen of England — from a superb private governess — but we were hard put to it to buy the few text books I needed for examinations. Academically I could not have been more fortunate, but socially I was to reap a very lonely harvest.

At the time, however, I was never conscious of being isolated. There was all that homework, set and voluntary. I didn't really want other kids of my own age to knock around with; once again I had outgrown my own generation. I was in Judy Garland's "in-between" stage for a long, long time, emotionally ready for adult relationships, socially ineligible. But I was content to bide my time.

Despite all the problems at home, Mother and I had our moments of fun and the bond was close. In the evenings I would dress up and perform my Shakespeare plays or act out chapters of history, or put on a one-girl concert for her. At Christmas there were still little gifts and nice things to eat, even though there were only the two of us to share them. The cinema was cheap then — even we could afford a weekly visit. On my fourteenth birthday, I fished a fairy-bun out of the tin and stuck fourteen matchsticks round it to represent candles. Something got through to her that time, for the next year there was a cake for me with fifteen candles, though she still could not face a party and I had to cut it up and take it round to my friends. This was one of many little incidents which eventually made me realise that it was sometimes apathy rather than sheer poverty which deprived us of things.

When Mother was having one of her "bad do's", as I called them, I was shattered and distressed and would cry for hours. There was nothing I could do for her — she could not be nursed or fed or cared for like a physically sick person. Precisely because I loved her so much and knew what a fine person she really was, this distortion of her personality was unbearable, and the fact that she would never let me send for the doctor terrified me, as she sometimes seemed so ill. One could never afford to shrug and say, "there she goes again, crying wolf!"

I know exactly why it is so difficult for teachers and neighbours to spot child abuse, especially the emotional kind. In the mornings, I would drag myself out of the house feeling as though all the troubles in the world were weighing me down, eyes stinging from the night's weeping and lack of sleep. But as I approached the school gate, the weight would lift, and I felt that I was entering a different world. This "two worlds" syndrome was to remain with me throughout the whole time we were living together. Without it, my school and office work, and all my outside pursuits, would have been impossible.

It seems terrible to use the term "abuse" when my poor mother was, in fact, so loving, so caring, so helpless; but I did suffer badly as a result of her seeming determination to create a one-to-one relationship with me, and to keep everyone else at a polite arm's length, including, of course, all the people who could have helped us so much. I think she had latterly been trying to do this with Father, too, and possibly with others before that. But what she failed to realise was that if her "one-to-one" person was sufficiently extrovert and sociable to do the things she expected of them — to earn the living and deal with all the business matters she could not face, and, in short, to act as a kind of "minder" to her rather than a partner or companion — then that person was not going to be satisfied with just a one-to-one relationship with her.

If my teacher had harboured any hopes that ways and means might be found to send me on to some kind of higher education, they were quickly dashed. I took a crash course in shorthand and typing at the cheapest little business school I could find and was at work in an office two months after my sixteenth birthday. I was paid twenty-five shillings a week — not much even in those days, but it helped, and at least I had stopped costing money. I had to fix up the course entirely by myself, and although it was "good practice for me", I realise now that a normal parent would not have left it all to a fifteen-year-old. The two terms cost just six guineas, and I left without so much as an RSA certificate to my name.

Rather sadly, I have to record that my teacher, who had done such a magnificent job while I was actually under her tuition, made something of a psychological error after I left. We kept up a correspondence, naturally enough, for we had been very close during those tense years of concentrated study, and she could not resist nit-picking at every spelling mistake and misjudgement of style or punctuation I made, even in the most hurried, informal, note — my visual memory was never so good as my aural recall. I knew she was right, and that she was only trying to help, but at that stage I really needed encouragement and reassurance more than I needed right-putting, and this drip-feed of criticism worried and upset me as I started to look for work. I was so young, I was so tired — we had not had a proper holiday in years — I was anaemic, and starting a job was a big challenge.

I had reached puberty before I was twelve, and although it is only a natural function, it eats a big chunk out of a little girl's childhood when it comes as early as that. By the time I was facing all these responsibilities I was drained of iron, and, again, in normal circumstances medical advice would have been sought. Mother fed me well, and dosed me with great beakers of Sanatogen, but avoided the involvement of taking me for a check-up.

Like the young people of the 1980's, I grew up in the shadow of unemployment — an additional worry. Then the war started and I stepped out into a labour market crying out for pairs of hands, however young and inexperienced. I was offered the first job for which I applied.

By my reckoning, as the sole consistent breadwinner of the household, I became a Senior Citizen from that day onward.

IN NO-MAN'S-LAND

In my early days, it was taken for granted that I was going to be a "career girl". Marriage was having a bad Press at the time, and the single, independent business-woman was envied by her housebound sister — even though in those days "single" really did mean totally celibate! If you were bright, and had parents who were able and willing to educate you, you were fortunate indeed. As soon as Father died, however, and the family became more or less estranged, I realised that there was going to be no money for higher education or proper vocational training, and that my best chance of a decent life-style would come through marriage. Besides, being a jolly bachelor auntie when you had brothers and sisters and there were little nieces and nephews growing up round you was one thing, but remaining single when you were as bereft of blood-relations as I was did not seem nearly so attractive.

The impression that little boys were made of frogs and snails soon gave way to romantic thoughts, fed by the cinema and popular literature. When the final pieces in the facts-of-life jigsaw began dropping into place, however, the picture which emerged was not at all to my liking. Sex, compared with the longed-for courtship, sounded such a frightening thing — a great painful leap from beauty to ugliness, from grace to indignity, from tenderness to violent invasion, leading to the stomach-churning miseries of pregnancy and the horrors of the the delivery-ward. The answer, I decided, must be love — when you met the right person, it would all look completely different. All around me, after all, were happy, dignified women who had survived the honeymoon and even the maternity unit.

I have since wondered how on earth the schools of those days managed to teach us quite advanced botany and biology and introduce us to all that passionate classical history and literature without clueing us up on human reproduction in the process, but somehow they did. Our generation were supposed to be much more free and enlightened than the previous one had been; we were allowed to read whatever we liked, including the Sunday papers, but no direct attempt was made at sex education, and in my case, with no playground gossip to supplement the *News of the World*, it took quite a long time for the final penny to drop. They say, too, that we invariably treat our own children in the same way that our parents treated us. Would I, therefore, like my mother before me, have dreaded and rejected my children in the antenatal abstract, but cared for them and grown to love them deeply when they arrived?

Despite this ambivalent attitude, my expectations when I emerged from the classroom into the office were that I should not be there for long. It was not that I had any illusions that I would be God's gift to the young men of the district, but I had been led to believe that unless you had two heads, you had some matrimonial value just by being a girl. There was no formal dowry system in Britain — in fact, if you had any money or expectations, you were warned to look out for fortune-hunters, so being hard up seemed no barrier.

Oddly enough, it never occurred to me that my mother's health problems might be off-putting. To begin with, I imagined that all the early stages of courtship would take place outside the home (literally "going out together") and that by the time it became necessary to introduce the young man, the emotional bond would be so strong that any snags like that would be brushed aside. I even had a kind of *Mills and Boon* daydream of marrying a young doctor, au fait with new methods, who would diagnose Mum's ills in a flash and bulldoze her into the right treatment before she realised what was happening. In any event, it was all supposed to be caused by worry, and the theory was that if and when circumstances improved, so would she.

My social isolation, I considered, was actually an advantage; no heavy father grumbling when I came in late, no pretty sisters to pinch my boy-friends, no nasty little brothers or catty old school-friends to tell tales. Footloose and fancy-free, with sufficient education to make me an interesting companion but not enough to turn me into a formidable blue-stocking, I felt thoroughly eligible. I thought that merely by moving around and having my being in the community, going to work, attending a church, using the buses and shops, cafes and theatres, I would automatically make contact with a cross-section of people of all types and backgrounds, and would quickly fall in with a group of young men and women of my own age and begin "dating" in the usual way. Indeed, I still feel that this is how a normal, heterogeneous Western society should operate.

It did not work out like that at all. I found myself in a social No-Man's-Land, an oddly compartmentalised society in which I had no place. Each stratum of that society appeared to consist of a nexus of communities, some large, like the fishing and dockland populations, others small, like the cluster of academics around the college which was to evolve into Hull University, but all centred on a trade, industry or profession. On our arrival in the area, of course, we had slipped automatically into one of those compartments — that of the Planemakers — but now we had no point of contact with any of them.

The huge working population were for the most part proud, insular and strongly resistant to change, but there was an upwardly mobile element which provided much of the managerial and entrepreneurial force in the leading industries of the region such as fishing, timber, paint-making and farming. Perhaps this was why there seemed to be so little young, male participation in the social and cultural life of the area, for if the interests of the manually-working lad centred on beer and football, those of the young executive differed only in that they focused on gin and golf (or he had his own boat or kept his own horse). In other words, it was still booze and sport; you never saw him at a theatre, a concert or a public lecture, however illustrious the speaker; he never bought a ticket for an organised event. Apart from those visits to up-market hostelries, mostly in the rural areas, his social round consisted of private functions, "twenty-firsts", engagement parties and the like.

The professional families mostly sent their children, especially the sons, away to be educated, then on to some form of vocational training, even if they were not bright enough to make it to university or polytechnic, after which they took jobs and settled in other parts of the country, leaving a permanent gap in the community. I now recall that none of the youngsters I played and learnt with between the ages of eight and twelve had older siblings at home during term-time. Their teenage brothers and sisters — actor Ian Carmichael was one of them — were all away at boarding school and appeared only briefly during the holidays, when they were vague, shadowy figures of which we little ones were in awe. Even when the university and the other colleges began to develop, there was little Town-and-Gown interaction — and student participation, again, seemed to be confined to pubs, pubs, pubs!

The effect of this kind of social structure is that there is virtually no *public* boy-meets-girl set-up, particularly for the better-educated. If one was not on the private party circuit, one had little chance of getting to know young people of one's own age and background, especially boys. I joined clubs, classes and societies and attended events of all kinds, at every social level, but although I met some delightful people, several friendships lasting to this day, none of these gatherings provided the young, lively, mixed company I was looking for. If one went to a dance, for instance — surely the quintessence of "respectable" courtship springboards in a normal community! — one had to take one's own partner, or one didn't get on the floor all evening.

Needless to say, I was not the only girl of my generation who was feeling this particular kind of draught. My whole nubile period, in fact, coincided with an international sex-imbalance, and much was heard about the "surplus woman". Added to the ever-present factor of the greater vulnerability of boys, who, despite improved paediatric medicine, still tend to be more adventurous and therefore at greater risk than girls, we were, for the second time this century, plunged into a world war, and although civilians shared the danger from air raids, it was still the male population who bore the brunt. In Russia, for instance, women found themselves mending roads and laying bricks, less in the cause of equality than because the slaughter of Stalingrad and other battles left too few men to do the work. Here in Britain, casualties were particularly heavy in the very age-group from which I and my contemporaries would normally have drawn our partners — the men about five or six years our seniors.

It is sometimes said that it is good for society when women are in the majority, for we are the peacemakers, the carers, the preservers of life; but my experience suggests the contrary. Women are able to exert their strongest influence when they are in the minority, and they do it all with the little word "no". When a man has to set his stall out to attract a nice partner, it brings out the manly, protective, hard-working best in him; when we are ten-a-penny, he can get away with murder. I attribute a lot of the blame for plummeting moral standards to the numerical surplus of women — or shortage of men — during this period, and the feminist lobby can make what they like of my theories!

I was not alone, either, in finding myself in a strange social trap. For me, of course, there had been no choice, but quite a number of girls of my generation, having gained good matric results, opted to go into office work rather than to continue their studies. They were honest enough to admit that they saw their future mainly in terms of home and family; they did not want parents to make financial sacrifices and teachers to waste their time training them for professions they did not intend to pursue for very long, and they felt it unfair to take up precious places which would be better filled by boys or career-minded girls. Some undoubtedly feared the bluestocking label.

But ironically, we were already too well-educated to fit in with the social scene I have just described. We had, without realising it, gone beyond the point of no return. If we had gone on to higher education we would have had the best of both worlds — a properly structured career and, at the same time, a much better chance of living, working and studying among our peers and forming compatible relationships, for, with more girls at colleges and universities, the men were becoming less chauvinistic, discovering that brains and sex-appeal were not incompatible. As it was, we had fallen for the worst of both worlds — a more-or-less dead-end job and a social life in which we had all too little chance of meeting a suitable partner. As Oscar Wilde might have put it, we were educated beyond our means.

Throughout my childhood, when my hyper education-conscious relatives had got together, I had heard it repeated time and again that the one legacy parents could leave their children which no-one could take from them was education; and the logical rider to that would seem to be that the more education one was given, the better, even if it could not go all the way. In practice, we were discovering that a little learning could be not only a dangerous thing but in some situations a socially divisive one, placing the semi-educated in a vacuum.

By my reckoning, the brain-drain from North to South must have been going on since long before Samuel Johnson saw the best prospect for the young Scot as being the road to England, and it was particularly acute in the little shirt-tail of Yorkshire then known as the East Riding. Even the region's greatest sons, such as William Wilberforce, had to spend most of their working lives in and around London, while Andrew Marvell did not waste much time complaining by the tide of Humber either, but hot-saddled it to the capital to continue his political and poetic activities there. I suppose this drift must have begun about the time of Alfred the Great, when England first began to be a recognisable country with London as its capital, rather than a group of little kingdoms; and, of course, it has always claimed the brightest and the best — and those who have not yet acquired family ties.

For some of my friends it was not too late. They left their office desks and went back to college. In other cases, parents who did not have a very sociable background nevertheless tumbled to the situation and helped their daughters to get away to places where they would find better opportunities and more balanced, congenial company. Lad-mad girls and matchmaking mums may seem like figures out of a Jane Austen novel, but my friend of the marriage bureau says that one of the things which keeps her in business is the fact that families do not help their young people in this way any more. It is surely not meddling or manipulating if parents keep an eye on the patterns of the society in which they are bringing up their young people and help them to overcome any difficulties of this nature?

It is often said that when one door shuts, another opens. I have found the opposite to be the case. When one door shuts it can start a chain reaction — slam, slam, slam! My inability to find a boy-friend, or even the most casual occasional escort, seemed to have a knock-on effect on my other relationships. A normal, heterosexual girl can be jolly good buddy-mates with another normal, heterosexual girl — but only up to a point. A single girl can have a very nice friendship with a married couple or family — but only up to a point. Three, five, seven and so on are all crowds. I had some super girl friends, and I know we could have been even closer to each other if we had met as members of a mixed peer group. We could have run around in foursomes and sixsomes, having fun for years before the serious pairing-off started. We could have been bridesmaid and best man for each other, our kids could have grown up together, we could have baby-sat for each other and gone on hilarious camping and caravan holidays in the early, hard-up days before we could afford hotels. We could have cried on each other's shoulders when things went wrong. I saw it happen with others and was envious.

The job I had taken with a firm of yeast merchants turned out to be less of a dead-end than it appeared to be at first. The call-up was already biting into the work-force, and after a few months as an invoice clerk I found myself handling a complex ledger system, working an accounting machine and typing the correspondence for the book-keeping department (known as the "B-K"). In short, I was doing three jobs for much less than the price of one. Looked at in one way, I was being grossly exploited, but I was gaining valuable experience which in peacetime would have taken years to achieve. I was also conscious that my cousins and neighbourhood acquaintances were all working just as hard at school or college, and were still beholden to their parents for every penny they spent. At least I had a measure of independence, while the freedom from homework and exam pressure, which, despite my love of learning, had latterly become far too much of a good thing, was welcome.

I got on quite well with my fellow workers, especially the older ones, who were very kind, understanding and encouraging. To the younger ones, however, I must have seemed a right oddball! With a posh address, a cut-glass accent and a head stuffed with classical allusions, I was nevertheless churchmouse skint, more than a little scruffy, and totally clueless when it came to everyday girl-talk and social intercourse. Looking back, I am surprised they tolerated me as well as they did.

During this period, I received a great deal of help and solace from membership of a Methodist Church. Aside from the spiritual aspect, the people there gave me friendship and provided invaluable outlets for writing and speaking. I can never be grateful enough to them — even though their society still did not offer the boy-meets-girl openings that I needed so badly, and I always had to walk home alone through the black-out and the air-raid alerts.

Neighbours, with one exception, were as kind as they could be in the circumstances, but there was little they could offer. When you are poor in a poor district, it is a unifying thing; you share what you have and it is all matey and friendly. But when you are grimly hard-up in a fairly affluent district, it cannot but be divisive. There is no way that rich and poor can socialise on equal terms without patronage, as I was to discover years later when I became interested in links between developed and Third World countries.

The war levelled things up a lot while it lasted, of course; we were all on equal rations, having to make do and mend, save fuel, do without cars, holidays and other luxuries, while most households were missing their menfolk, anyway. But there was still a barrier.

BACK TO SQUARE ONE

The war ended. We had lost nobody — we had nobody to lose. By the time peace came I was mature enough to realise the absurdity of our continuing to live as we were doing. The house may arguably have saved our lives — I can still remember the red glow in the sky under a great, rolling bank of plum-coloured smoke as the centre of Hull burned to death in the Blitz of May 1941 — but the property was eating its own tail, having had to be mortgaged to enable us to keep going, and it was now badly in need of repair and decoration.

The company for which I worked owned some old town properties which were being roughly converted into flats, and I was lucky to be able to get one to rent, in view of the desperate housing shortage. We moved into the flat, the house was sold and the money invested to provide a small income. After all those years, our money problems were virtually at an end. But as we left the village, a line from Browning's *"Andrea del Sarto"* kept echoing in my head; "...the melancholy little house we built to be so gay with".

Although the flat was tatty, I revelled in the new situation. It was great to be able to see a play right through at the theatre without having to leave early to catch the last bus out to the village. At a pinch we could have walked home now. I took up new interests, and eventually got a new and much better job, which I would have found difficult to manage if I had still had to face the long bus rides. The men returning from the Forces had naturally been given their jobs back, and my former employers did not really know what to do with the girls who had kept the seats warm during their absence, so we found ourselves relegated to any little dogsbody tasks around the office.

The new job was in a newspaper office, so I was one jump nearer to what I had always wanted — something to do with words and writing, though I would never have dared to breathe the word "journalism" in my teacher's hearing, as this would have unleashed an immediate spate of reminders about my current batch of spelling mistakes. It was with great joy that I later discovered that Winifred Holtby couldn't spell either. I wish I had known it then!

My secretarial duties were varied with all sorts of social events, helping to run a horse show, gala queen competitions, big charity balls and other functions, and I loved it. I had been warned that this was no job for a clock-watcher, but I didn't mind the extra hours at all. Once again, it was hard to say where work ended and fun began. In short, I was using the flat as a mere *pied-à-terre,* and its dilapidations did not trouble me. It was inexpensive and I could find much better uses for the extra cash than spending it on elegant surroundings. All around, people were celebrating the peace in a way which rather mirrored the beautiful Jewish feast of Chanukah, bringing out the last of their meagre resources to light up the darkness and banish the obscenities of war. Shabby, bomb-damaged rooms were packed with party guests sitting on cushions on the floor because there were not enough chairs, drinking beer out of cracked cups and mugs because there were no glasses.

I had expected my mother to follow the same line as myself, taking up creative interests, finding new friends, making a new and independent life for herself, even, perhaps, looking for a little job, for shops and businesses were crying out for assistants, and were more than pleased to employ older women for their greater experience and *savoir-faire.* But for her the move had been something of frying-pan-into-fire experience. The shabbiness of the property depressed her and she soon began falling out with the other tenants. It became a vicious circle; she felt too poorly to do anything positive, and the longer she sat looking at the leprous distempered walls and crooked door frames (the district was riddled with subsidence) and listening to the couple upstairs playing "Moonlight and Roses" on the gramophone to drown the noise of their latest shouting match, the worse she felt.

She had a point, I had to admit. The area had been designed for the upper end of the fishing industry — the skippers and mates — and the houses had originally been very fine, but the coming of the car had heralded a movement out to the suburbs and the street was now sliding down-market with growing impetus. When we first moved in, some of the neighbours had been people of our own ilk, but they gradually left as the housing shortage eased. In hot weather we had to sprinkle cologne on our pillow to kill the smell of the fish-manure factory which pervaded the whole of West Hull; by night, the sound of revellers returning full-bellied and full-throated from the pubs made sleep a fitful thing.

There was, however, a famous Rugby League ground nearby, and although this drew great crowds, I must say that we never had the slightest trouble from them. It was, and is, a well-mannered sport in spite of its robust image.

I cannot be sorry that Britain lost the Cod War. The long-distance trawling industry was a cruel and greedy one, in which the young and untrained were exploited and money was often more important than men's lives. It offered none of the compensations which merchant seafaring, for all its rigours, brings — the visits to foreign ports, the pleasures of "dipping through the tropics by the palm-green shores" — just cold and darkness and boredom and deadly peril. The lines of communication were too stretched, and trawlermen, if they were lucky, often took refuge in Icelandic ports, where they were invariably succoured and well treated in spite of any political animosity raging at the time.

The industry bred a negative kind of culture in which there was admittedly a lot of generosity and mutual aid, but it went hand-in-hand with waste and apathy. Apart from a few local superstitions, there seemed to be little, if any, folk-lore in the way of handed-down songs, stories or crafts such as are found in other fishing communities, and there was quite a lot of domestic violence. Yet there was always this stubborn resistance to change, and when, after the war, boys and girls were urged to take up their educational opportunities, all too many still opted for the status quo.

Nevertheless, I was reluctant to start looking for alternative accommodation, and still more unwilling to take on the responsibilities of owning a house in the area. I really wanted to get away altogether, for by now I had realised that demobilisation had not restored balance to the social scene. The brain-drain had in fact accelerated; in good times, the best jobs were elsewhere, in bad times, the only jobs were elsewhere. Able young people flitted through my world from time to time, but it was clear that the last thing they wanted to do was to put down roots here and form serious relationships. True, I was enjoying my work and my leisure-time interests, but I still found myself echoing Dorothy Parker's words " — I don't pretend these fill my life; at least they fill my time."

Eventually, however, something had to be done. Mother began to be really ill. The "bad do's" came thick and fast, and this time she seemed to be ailing physically as well. I took the small legacy I had received from my grandmother's estate, added most of my savings and put down a deposit on a suburban terraced house. It was a nice little house with "capabilities", as Lancelot Brown might have put it, for modernisation, while the repayments and upkeep were well within my reach. I reconciled myself to the fact that I was now more closely tied to the district, but I was still in my twenties — just — and there was always the hope that something, or someone, might turn up.

At first, the change seemed to have done the trick. Some months later, however, I came home to find that another "bad do" had started. I remember sobbing like a child. What was it now? We had a decent home of our own and no financial worries, so what more could be done? We were back to Square One.

Poor Mum had run out of excuses and scapegoats. She tried to blame trivial upsets or old age or to claim that it was all part of the normal wear and tear of life: "I can't always be well, you know!" But it didn't wash with me any more, and from then onwards our relationship began to deteriorate. The fact that there was now a National Health Service meant that she need not fear doctor's bills any more, but although I pleaded with her to seek medical help, she still refused, and I became really angry at her complacency, her willingness to allow the Demon Neurosis — for that, to be fair, was what it really was — to dominate and spoil both our lives in this way.

Like Dylan Thomas, I wanted my parent at least to "rage, rage against the dying of the light" — not the light of life itself in this instance, but of all the things which, to me, made it worth living: creative activity, outreach to other people, "laughter and the love of friends".

After a session, she always seemed to be able to pull down a kind of mental shutter, blotting out the memory and behaving as though it had never happened. Those who like colourful tags might call it the Dorian Gray Syndrome — this ability to take all the ugly, unpleasant things about oneself and lock them away in a kind of mental attic, opening the door now and then to peer briefly in and contemplate with horrid fascination the ever-worsening record. Up to that time, I suppose I had done pretty much the same; it was all part of that "two worlds" illusion. Now it didn't work any more.

In some ways, we had become like one of those couples who marry in hard times and get along splendidly together all the while they have nothing; but as soon as their circumstances start to improve, the cracks begin to appear. Sometimes it is the poor little wife who turns out to be "shy" and cannot face meeting people, or who cannot get used to spending money. Sometimes the husband is the old stick-in-the-mud who doesn't want to go on holiday or move to a better house, who cannot be poured into a decent suit or prised from his armchair, his pipe and his sports page. One of the most tragic aspects of this situation is the retrospective reversal of perception that it brings; what previously seemed like courage and fortitude is now seen as cowardice, what seemed like patience and forebearance now looks like dullness and apathy, what seemed like thrift becomes a maddening miserliness.

The thirty-six year age gap between my mother and myself was another handicap. She had only to say, "Wait until you get to my age!" and I was left without an answer. How, indeed, would I cope with the menopause when it came, or with the limitations of the advancing years? And by the time I had reached the one, she was well into the next stage. At sixty, of course, she became a statistic — an "elderly" relative for whom society would expect me to accept responsibility. When we reached that landmark, I was not quite twenty-four.

Except for rare moments of truth, usually when she was coming out of an attack, and when she agonisingly faced the situation as it was for a brief spell, I think she told herself that she was doing a useful job keeping house for her business-girl daughter, who had wisely chosen the better part by remaining single and free. She could not seem to understand that, job or no job, husband and kids or no husband and kids, any girl with normal female instincts would, by the age of eighteen or so, have been longing for her own place, even if it was only a student bed-sitter with a gas-ring where she could fry sausages for her cronies.

Aside from our personal problems, we found ourselves in a trap which must be well known in all cases of stay-at-home daughters: who does what when visitors come? You cannot expect Mum to go on year after year slaving over a hot stove to feed your friends, yet you cannot turn her out of a woman's most sacrosanct domain, her kitchen. Usually, I believe, in such cases the older woman takes the lead, establishing a routine for visiting friends or family or attending some kind of meeting so that her daughter can have the house to herself on a regular basis, but with my mother unable to face any kind of organised social activity, that avenue was closed to me.

With facilities for bringing friends home so restricted, I found it difficult to sustain relationships. Most people seemed to understand, but many must have wondered why I never invited them home. Several times I thought we had achieved a breakthrough, and I even set up a rather pathetic bedsitter arrangement at one stage, but it never really worked.

There was, I admit, a lot of commonsense thrift in my mother's economies, and I learned much from her, which I still put into practice, but her reluctance to accept sensible improvements in our standard of living as our income rose was often extremely trying, and it became increasingly obvious that her objections frequently arose from irrational fears rather than from reasoned argument.

Luckily, I had my "other world", and here things were moving in an unexpected direction. Almost by chance I had started filtering over into the newspaper's editorial department. I did copious stints of telephone copy-taking from reporters in the field — an excellent way of learning how seasoned newsmen and women work and think. I landed little overspill jobs from the News Editor's diary — film reviews, amateur play productions and school shows nobody else wanted to do. I wrote paragraphs for the diary columns and, encouraged by their acceptance, longer articles for the weekly series issued from the same office. This was why, in later years, I always voted against the Closed Shop; if one had been in operation, I would never have got into journalism.

Finally, it was agreed that I would be more useful in this area, and I officially became a journalist. I did not dare to tell my dear old teacher for a long time. She would have tried so hard to "help" by tearing my early published efforts to shreds, and I needed all the confidence I could muster. I have often wondered whether my acceptance as a journalist on a fast evening newspaper, unqualified as I was and well over the normal age for entry, represented the reverse side of the brain-drain coin. Precisely because of the shortage of qualified young people willing to settle and work in the North, maybe the less qualified picked up jobs and opportunities they would not otherwise have got. After all, there had to be something good about it!

I was never any great shakes as a news reporter. Apart from the fact that I had entered the craft too late for proper training and had not had the usual baptism of working on a country weekly, I don't think I had the temperament for it. My forte was features and the straight reporting of events. In those halcyon days, provincial newspapers really tried to reflect the community in which they operated, systematically recording the activities of all the established organisations, so there was plenty that a person like myself, who had always had a certain facility with words, could do to make those reports agreeably readable. I interviewed visiting celebrities, covered all kinds of functions and generally made myself useful. I even enjoyed writing advertisement features — anathema to most journalists — finding them quite a challenge. On one occasion, I wrote the copy for an entire holiday supplement in rhymed couplets — and the Editor accepted it!

When finally turned loose on the municipal scene, I discovered a facility — Horace Walpole might have called it Serendipity — for chancing upon strange little stories on such unlikely assignments as the Cleansing and Sanitary or Markets and Abattoirs Committees. One of these, back in the 1960's, was an all-time commentary on the "Affluent Society". The Corporation, it emerged, had encountered quite a problem in dealing with large items of furniture, including beds, sideboards, wardrobes and three-piece suites, which had been dumped on the sides of roads or in the open drains which then abounded in the city, as *nouveau-riche* dockers refurbished their homes.

Sometimes, perhaps on account of my BBC accent rather than my sex, I would be used on "sensitive" stories such as breaking the news to a murderer's wife that her husband had received a life-sentence, interviewing a girl who was still in shock after seeing her husband shot down on the infamous "Murder Mile" in Cyprus, or following up missing-child stories.

I did a good deal of political reporting and met some of the leading figures of the Sixties — Hugh Gaitskell, Bessie Braddock, a great, warm, lovely character, and Enoch Powell, whose piercing eyes and compelling rhetoric were always frighteningly convincing even before he raised the spectre of uncontrolled immigration. On one occasion, while her husband was Prime Minister, Lady Dorothy Macmillan actually brought her speech forward by a few minutes at my request, so that we could catch an early edition — a charming example of *noblesse oblige*.

Music and drama, both amateur and professional, provided some of my most enjoyable assignments. As theatre critic over a five-year period, I saw a range of shows, from the splendid to the awful, and met a host of stars. Two whom, I remember with particular affection were the 6ft comedian Cardew Robinson, who used to do an act as an overgrown schoolboy with cap and scarf, yet proved off-stage to be one of the most interesting and intelligent show-business characters I ever interviewed; and Charlie Chester, who, discovering that I had an extremely bad cold, bought me a brandy and Babysham, which he vowed was an infallible cure — it certainly made life look rosier!

I remember being taught Cockney rhyming slang by Ronald Shiner and regaled with saucy-but-nice stories in a delicious Scottish accent by Renee Houston. Renee was a very moral lady who hated smut, and she always liked coming to Hull because the theatre was only yards away from the beautiful church of St. Charles. "I'm an old sinner, but I do love my faith", she would say.

The amateur theatre, however, was my favourite. There was the tiny Janus Theatre established by Stella Sizer-Simpson and her company in an old church building in the heart of the fishing community; there were the Garret Players, who swept the board at festivals, the long-established Playgoers, the village dramatic societies and those based on local industries. There were formidable producers such as Hannchen Drasdo and Phyllis Sharrah, who boomed and bullied fine performances out of rabbit-scared tiros. And there were those wonderful school performances during the ripe era when, under that superb English teacher, John Large, Kingston High School became a veritable "Fame" academy, producing such actors as Tom Courtenay and John Alderton.

It was at Newland High School that I "discovered" Maureen Lipman, now one of Britain's top actresses. She was playing the title role in Marlowe's *"Faustus"*, and although she was magnificent throughout the whole, long, poetry-drenched play, it was her final exit that convinced me of her potential. Dragged off to Hell by two she-devils, her feet trailing pitifully, she emitted a long, terrified howl that truly merited the description "blood-curdling". For a twelve year-old to act so uninhibitedly in the presence of parents, teachers and fellow-pupils seemed to me to argue a remarkable degree of concentration and identification with a role. My overnight copy began with the words; "Maureen Lipman — remember that name!" I was told off by the News Editor for going over the top about a mere school performance which could not have been all that good. It was unwise, I was reminded, to put ideas into the heads of little schoolgirls... But fortunately it was too late: the paper was out and Maureen was on her way to stardom.

Of the "serious" musicians I met, one of the easiest to interview was Sir John Barbirolli, a charming man who loved conducting for Northern audiences and had no illusions about culture stopping at Watford. Benjamin Britten appeared painfully shy and was difficult to draw out, but warmed slightly when I asked his views on music for children. At the ceremony following the interview, the person playing *"God Save the Queen"* seemed unable to hit the right note, and I do not think that mine was the only face that registered pained embarrassment. Then, all was explained: it was, of course, Dr Britten's own arrangement of the National Anthem!

Eventually, I was appointed Woman Editor, a post which, I discovered, went far beyond the compiling of a daily column of chit-chat about local girls in the news, the latest club activities or features on food and fashion. Largely because of precedents set by some of my predecessors, who had been truly remarkable women with strong characters, I found chunks of social commentary creeping in, and quite often these got me into trouble with readers who found my views less than compassionate.

It is, however, all too easy to win quick popularity by taking the conventional line, always speaking up for the under-dog, and this was something I was never willing to do if I felt that the dog could do more to help himself. Perhaps it was precisely because I had come through such a tough time myself that I was able to see through so many of the hard-luck stories I was pitched. The Welfare State, especially in the early years of my editorship, really did seem to be caring for most material needs if one knew one's way around it, and I quickly detected a tendency to expect the system to do everything, even solving problems which were way outside its mandate.

I like to think, however, that my feature did help the local and national charities in many ways by publicising their activities, that it provided a shop-window for the clubs and societies which were offering a service to the community, and, in particular, that it did what it could to help solve this dreadful problem of loneliness. It helped to start many self-help groups and singles clubs, which brought companionship to scores of people, even though it could do nothing to right the balance of the sexes. It also brought together a large number of "lost" relatives, friends, former neighbours and wartime comrades — besides, on occasion, replacing other kinds of loss, too.

I was reminded quite recently by one of the North of England's brightest artists, soprano Jean Ward-Skerrow, of the time when she poured out to me the sorry tale of how some irreplaceable sheet music, and her best evening dresses, had been stolen from her car while she was keeping an engagement in West Yorkshire. I wrote the story, and before the ink was dry, Jean had received dozens of offers of copies of the much-loved out-of-print ballads which had been in the stolen music-case — to say nothing of a whole wardrobe of loaned evening gowns! The heart-warming story of how little old ladies had searched through their cupboards for half-forgotten copies of the songs they had sung round the parlour piano when they were girls illustrates, I think, a very strong characteristic of life in this North Eastern town — this nostalgic tenderness for the past. Among the most popular items my colleagues and I used over the years were pictures of events which took place 50 and more years before, and which brought back memories, happy or poignant.

Although my feature was not supposed to be an "agony column" as such, there was a long-standing tradition that the occupant of my chair was a friend to whom readers, male or female, could pour out their troubles and receive some kind of response, often by correspondence or personal interview. Sometimes, those troubles made my own seem insignificant.

One day I was interviewing a young woman who was trying to start a self-help group for families beset by Huntington's Chorea. She told a heartbreaking story about her mother, who was a victim of this horrible condition. The father could not stand it any longer — and walked out. The elder sister could not stand it any longer — and walked out. Still only a child herself, my caller had been left to cope alone, and as she described how her mother had gone into bouts of violence and had on more than one occasion set the house on fire, I felt, not for the first time, like the person with no shoes looking at the person with no feet.

DOUBLE LIFE

Nevertheless, as the work situation improved, the strange dichotomy of my life was thrown into stark relief. I had become something of a local "front" figure, in demand for giving talks, sitting on panels, judging competitions, responding to toasts and opening charity events — a plump-ish little fish in a parochial pool, if you like. Yet I never knew what I was going home to.

I got to know literally hundreds of people, and several became my very valued friends. I was invited to join the Soroptimist Club — the women's equivalent of Rotary — where I found a real spirit of sisterhood. Yet none of the people I knew were in a position to help resolve my problems, or share the ups and downs in any close and intimate way. They all had their own homes, families, circles of friends of long standing, and there was a strict limit to what I could ask, or expect them to do for me. Whenever I was sent two complimentary tickets for a function, I still had to throw one away every time, and the symbolism of this little action always hurt.

By now, I could afford to run a second-hand car, possessed a reasonable stock of clothes, though I was never very fashion-minded, and even managed to get away for a few mind-stretching overseas holidays and educational ventures, though a little cloud of anxiety hovered over me everywhere I went, and my emotions pulled two ways — longing, yet fearing, to get away from home.

Eventually, we moved to a new and better house — the small one needed re-wiring and extensive modernisation, and I knew that if this were set in hand it would be the signal for weeks of wretchedness and embarrassment, as Mother could not stand workmen in the house, even to do quite small repairs. Oddly enough, a removal and a complete new start somewhere else seemed to bring about a temporary remission, perhaps because the conscious effort of getting to know a new environment used up some of the spare adrenalin.

Sometimes, when I was downhearted, Mother would remind me of how well I had done, and of all the nice things I now possessed. "But don't you see?" I would reply with angry self-pity: "These are just the very things that the moralists and the do-gooders list, and then snap their fingers and say, 'These things don't matter THAT much! It's LOVE that counts — it's PEOPLE ROUND YOU!" It wasn't only a case of "You've got me but who have I got?" as I believe Groucho Marx once asked of an under-valued companion. Equally worrying was what would happen to her if I, who was living much more dangerously, had a fatal accident.

Maybe I was too prone to feel sorry for myself — indeed, there may be some who are by now quite nauseated by my self-pity, but I would ask them to remember that I am writing this account for a purpose, and am trying to be analytical rather than sympathy-seeking. Behind my griping, too, lay a curious commentary on the way we live today. It is constantly reiterated that we live in a materialistic society — but we don't. We live in a society with materialism, if you like, but if it was society itself that was materialistic, that society would condone materialism, the Establishment would applaud and advocate it as a desirable thing. And it doesn't. Every moral and cultural influence to which we are exposed from birth, from St Paul to the latest glossy American soap-opera, preaches the gospel of love, puts family life and friends before any other consideration, and denies us the right to enjoy any of the pleasures money, possessions and prestige can bring unless these things come as a bonus on top of loving relationships. It may be argued that the kind of love preached by St Paul was the outward-going variety, and point to such world-renowned humanitarians as Mother Theresa. All I can say in response to that is that all the members of celibate religious orders that I have met and conversed with seem to have a particularly rich, warm and strong bond with their families, even if they seldom actually see them. They can always tell you what O-levels their nephew is taking, which university their niece has just entered, and where Uncle Liam is going for his holidays this year!

While I am on this tack, we are constantly being told, too, that ours is a violent society, but the same applies: there is plenty of violence about, Heaven knows, but surely society itself has never been less violent? Never before has "the pomp and circumstance of glorious war" been so universally outlawed, especially by the young. Never before have our Western communities been without their gallant young officers, itching for a scrap to start somewhere in the world so that they can rush into battle and show off their courage and their smart uniforms. Never before has our penal system been so humane or our educational establishments so lax in discipline. This, of course, probably explains why so much of the violence has passed from the official to the criminal sector!

My lack of "ain folk" proved embarrassing in many small, subtle ways. When it became essential for me to learn to drive — no easy task, for co-ordination was never my strong point — I ruefully discovered that of all the dozens of people I knew who had cars, not one was sufficiently close for me to feel that I could ask them to give me some practice between lessons — and nobody volunteered. I passed the test at the second attempt, but I suspect that it was only because it was a miserably wet day, neither the examiner nor myself could really see properly, and the poor man probably felt he couldn't take any more waterworks from a failed woman driver, so he gave me the benefit of the doubt!

Some time later, I had to go into hospital for a fairly big operation, and made the distressing discovery of how awkward it could be not to have a viable next-of-kin or "next friend" to organise visiting and maintain contact with one's home base. Although my mother was in her seventies by this time, she was not officially ill or handicapped in any way, but her dread of using the telephone, especially if the call had to go through a switchboard, and of travelling by car or taxi, meant that I was almost completely cut off from the outside world, and I sensed that the hospital staff found it curious that a well-known local woman could find herself in that situation. Among my fellow patients were several girls from other towns who were studying at local colleges, and also one or two from overseas, but they all seemed to have some agency or group of colleagues swinging into action in place of their kinsfolk; I, who ostensibly had a home and a relative living locally had nothing to fall back on when those resources failed to respond. My emotions heightened by the shock of the operation, I found it humiliating to have to go to the hospital in a taxi and be taken home by ambulance because there was no one who could call for me. After all, I could not ignore the fact that I had grown up in the area and had tried very hard to integrate into the community.

One curious trend I have noticed — and I wonder whether it is shared by others — is that when you have a neurosis problem in the home, you seem to act as a positive magnet for other people with similar or related afflictions. This, I believe, puzzles psychiatrists, who cannot understand why the son or daughter of such a person so often seems deliberately to "choose" a partner or associate with the same characteristics. Believe me, it is not a question of choice!

The reasons are, indeed, difficult to pin down, especially since it is not a like-to-like attraction: it is the carer who is the target, not the afflicted relative, whose very existence may, in the first instance, be unknown to the newcomer.

What I think happens is this: neurotic people can, as I have shown, be very charming and attractive. Often, they seem more intelligent and accomplished than they are. They have a facility for picking up words and phrases from others, and are frequently clever mimics. New beginnings can bring about an improvement in their control for a time. They "sell" themselves very skilfully; they invariably have a plausible hard-luck story to tell of misunderstood genius. It is only when one gets to know them in some depth that one gradually realises how superficial it all is. They have a history of failure, in work and in relationships, and you eventually discover that you are only the latest in a long line of "props" on whom they have leaned.

Some that I encountered were absolute 20th century vampires, sucking their victims dry of energy — and sometimes of money, too, though I escaped that one! They can drain and exhaust any number of supporters, yet their own condition never changes. They are forever in dire trouble, yet they survive to batten on others, and their victims are often people like myself — people who are themselves functioning efficiently enough, and who may have a considerable amount of bottled-up affection to give, yet who lack the usual gamut of friends and relatives who, in normal circumstances, would prevent such exploitation from taking place. Indeed, a person living a normal family life simply would not have the time or the freedom to befriend such people so closely. Obviously, we who are out on a social limb because of our own problems must stick out like the proverbial chapel hat-pegs in the community, and sick personalities have no difficulty in homing in on us.

There were several common factors I noticed among the neurosis sufferers with whom I became linked. One was a tendency to ceaseless bragging — impressive at first, but one soon discovered how empty it was. It goes without saying that they were self-centred to the point of narcissism. This was attributed to inferiority complex, even by the people themselves, who would, when challenged, plead that they were "only doing it to convince themselves", and assert that they were not really as conceited as they sounded. But underneath, I detected a deeper conviction that they were, indeed, very special people with outstanding ability, and that if they could only straighten out their lives once and for all, the world would appreciate them for what they were. It may have been a simple case of delusions of grandeur...or was it?

In every instance, they claimed to be in some way "fey" — to have premonitions or psychic experiences of some kind or to have seen strange phenomena. I would be the last to dismiss these claims out of hand. It may very well be that these unfortunate people, with their abnormal brain-chemistry, are given a perception denied to the rest of us.

Neurosis sufferers often seem unable to learn from their mistakes or experiences. Failure always takes them by surprise, right from schooldays. One man I knew repeatedly talked his way into jobs which were way beyond his capabilities, and was invariably astonished and bewildered when he quickly lost them.

There were other lame dogs, too, for whom I had a lot of sympathy, but for whom I could do nothing. They were simply social misfits — people who were slightly above average intelligence for their class and background and had leanings towards cultural pursuits, yet who lacked the ability to acquire the polish and sophistication necessary to enable them to take their place in the circles to which they aspired, remaining unacceptably gauche and boring. Life can be hard for such folk; they fall between two stools and are doomed to loneliness too.

Psychiatrists and social workers constantly speak of the scars left on the personality of the trauma-victim — the inability to love, to trust, to form relationships. They never seem to consider the actual social scars, the fact that even if one remains emotionally sound, or manages to fight one's way through to normality, at the end of the day there may be no-one TO love, to trust, to relate to; no-one on whom one has any claim.

I must not love this man — he is my friend's husband. I must not monopolise that child — she is not mine. Always, always, this need to pull back, to put the brake on natural feelings, not only to observe the social niceties but to avoid hurting others.

A girl so soon reaches a stage in life when every man she meets is either married already, homosexual, or an unacceptable number of years younger than she is. A man still has much more social flexibility, and neither legislation nor custom can alter that. However, in middle life, one sometimes finds a kind of harvest season in which one meets chaps who are coming round for the second time. As I entered my forties, two or three promising relationships began to develop. Unfortunately, however, none of them got very far. There always seemed to be an old flame flickering away in the background whose claim was stronger than mine — or who, I suspect, could offer a more comfortable and open kind of background. It should not really have upset me as much as it did. It should have been a case of "we did have fun and no harm done". But, of course, in the circumstances I took it very badly indeed.

It may be wondered why I never turned to my friend of the marriage bureau, but by the time I got to know her I had realised that things were not going to get any better at home, and I felt it would be unfair to approach anyone in that way. By then my *Mills and Boon* character had changed to the modern equivalent of a knight in armour who would slash his way through the thicket, climb the tower and take me away from all this.

Quentin Crisp, in his sensitive exposé of the problems of transsexuality, wrote of his "great, dark man" — the ideal companion he had always dreamed of meeting. In the end, he realised that if this perfect specimen ever did turn up, he would not want Quentin Crisp — he simply would not be homosexual. It was the same with my "little, ugly interesting man", as I thought of him. If he was the sort of mature, warm, lovely person who would see in me a pilgrim soul he could cherish, it was nine pounds to the penny he would already be happily married. In fact, I rather suspect that men like that did cross my path from time to time, but, of course, by the time we met it was too late.

Very late in the day, I was in fact, briefly married, but perhaps the least said about that the better. It was not a case of "any old port in a storm" as might be imagined. It really did seem at first as though my luck had changed and we had both found the perfect partners for each other, but it was not to be: those old Fates still had some thunderbolts left up their togas. The best that can be said is that it all seems like a dream now; it was an episode that came and went and left not a rack behind.

It was during this time that my poor mother came to the end of the road. One night she upset a bedside lamp which set something smouldering and the room filled with smoke. She would have been ninety on her next birthday, but, sadly, there would have been no way in which we could have celebrated,even though she was still physically and mentally in good shape. If we had tried to take her out, or even to make a party for her in her own home, it would have been a nightmare she would have dreaded.

One day in May when she was eighty-five, I had come home excited: "Mum," I cried, "The cherry blossom is more beautiful than I have ever seen it. This is the moment the Japanese sit up all night waiting for, because it lasts such a short time. Put your coat on and hop in the car and I'll drive you round for a few minutes so that you can see it!" She refused, of course, with lame excuses, though she always loved flowers. "Mum," I went on, almost in tears, "Housman said, 'Now of my threescore years and ten, twenty will not come again'. You've had your threescore years and ten plus this wonderful bonus of fifteen, and you've still got perfect sight and hearing, but how many more spring days will you have to 'see the cherry hung with snow?'"

After her death I was strangely calm.It seemed that I had got all my grieving and weeping done years before. A week or two later, I was in the house packing things away as one has to do on these occasions. There was a bright little tune running through my head, and suddenly it was as though I heard her just behind me: "It's all right, Barbie — it's all right!" That was all. It was a young voice, excited, surprised. Then I recognised the tune that had played so persistently and incongruously in my mind: it was the *Merry Widow Waltz*. She and Father had danced to it when they first met.

Yes, of course it was only the subconscious back-projecting at an emotional time...or was it? As I have said, I have an open mind about such things. And I cannot rid myself of the feeling that somewhere, somehow she is living out the life she would have had if some biochemical wires had not become crossed at her conception.

How would she feel if she knew I was telling her story now? Strangely enough, despite her efforts to keep her pathetic secret between the two of us, she would sometimes say to me, when we were in the throes of a "bad do", "Just think, Barbie, what a splendid book you'll be able to write about all this one day!"

PART II — INTO AFRICA AND BEYOND

God knows, I never wanted it this way. I never wanted freedom and peace of mind to come through *losing* people. But that's the way it was in my crazily twisted cookie-crumble. I emerged from a long, dark tunnel to find myself with my own wee house, sufficient money to cushion me from worry, two tiny Yorkshire terriers for company, and my job.

One spring day, I was walking with the dogs through a wood. There were bluebells as far as the eye could see, with pink campion and delicate white wood-anemone for contrast, under a tracery of tender green leaves. Suddenly, I had a strange feeling. It was not a religious experience — at least, not directly — and yet it was much more than an aesthetic response to the beauty around me.

Quite simply, for the first time in my adult life I was appreciating something purely for its own sake. Not since the day I had left school and felt myself qualified for grown-up relationships had I been able to relish anything without having a compatible companion at my side to share it. The brighter the moonlight, the more lustrous the stars, the sweeter the scents, the more delicious the food, the finer the artistry, the more perfect the music, the more compelling the play, the more I had felt the aching emptiness within.

Now, standing in that hushed woodland, I had shed fifty years. I was five-years old again, looking at the sunset, gathering cowslips in a Gloucestershire meadow, watching the sparklers throwing out their rich, golden showers into the November night, with not a thought in my head other than the sheer bliss of the moment.

I had made a great discovery: loneliness is a terrible thing, but the worst form of loneliness is living with the wrong people.

What happened in the next five years was not planned — at least, not by me. While I was assiduously shaping my ends in the pursuit of those elusive "ain folk", that old divinity was rough-hewing them into a series of extraordinary experiences which I was to have the satisfaction of sharing with thousands of other people through writing and speaking.

In 1980, a "twinning" link was formed between Hull and Freetown, capital of Sierra Leone. Such links are, of course, by no means uncommon, but this one held a particular significance. Hull was the birthplace of William Wilberforce, whose long campaign to end the infamous slave traffic between the West Coast of Africa and the American colonies ended in triumph, and with poetic fitness, a few days before his death in 1833. Freetown was one of the communities established by the slaves who returned to their land of ethnic origin.

As part of the twinning ceremonies, the Mayor of Freetown, Dr June Holst-Roness, visited Hull, and I interviewed her for the newspaper. This beautiful and accomplished woman, who had won international recognition for her public work, made a deep impression on me, and when she said, "Why don't you visit my country?" I felt that it was more than a polite rhetorical question. Why not indeed?

I knew sufficient about provincial newspaper economics to realise that it would be useless to suggest making this an official assignment, notwithstanding the potential reader-interest, but there was no reason why I should not use my own holiday leave and money for the project. Packaged tours had long since palled, especially without a travelling companion; I had always ploughed interesting holiday experiences back into my column or into special feature articles or advertising supplements — ignoring criticism that in doing so without extra payment I was allowing my services to be exploited. Travel writing, re-living memorable sights and scenes and sharing them with others, always gave me tremendous pleasure, and now I had no-one to please but myself.

With the help of the newly-formed Hull-Freetown Society, and a lot of encouragement from the Guildhall, supported by "Dr June" herself, the plans were made, and one damp November day in 1981 I set off in my little green Polo for Gatwick. The long drive was the worst part of the journey, for, as I have said, I am an indifferent driver with a genious for getting on the wrong track, but, with the aid of a borrowed AA route, I made it in good time to board the British Caledonian plane bound for Lungi Airport, with a stop at Dakar, in Senegal.

Despite all the homework I had done on Sierra Leone itself, it speaks volumes for my general geographical knowledge that when I heard the first landing announced, I thought for a moment that I was in the wrong plane, believing Dakar to be in India! Little did I

Young Africa.

know as I hid my blushes that only four years later I was to be landing at Dhaka, which, is, of course, the capital of Bangladesh.

I love flying, although I can appreciate the frustrations of business people who are doing it all the time. I have never lost the little-girl thrill of eating ingeniously packaged meals thousands of feet above the earth, undoing all the miniature knives and forks and spoons, the little packets of salt and pepper. I don't even mind night flights, though I am usually too excited about the prospect before me to get much sleep.

When dawn broke, we were flying into a blazing red African sunrise, and as the plane landed and we boarded the coach, I began to understand the feelings of those Europeans who fall in love with this great Dark Continent and never want to leave it. That incredible red earth, the lush green foliage, the vivid flowers, the pungent smells, are strangely alluring. The people, too, in their infinite variety, are fascinating. No — they're not "just the same as we are". They are intriguingly, sometimes maddeningly and even saddeningly, different, and I think we get along best when we accept those differences and don't try to deny their existence.

As the coach drew in beside the ferry which was to take us across the bay to Freetown, my eyes were drawn to the stream of people gathering on the quay, some carrying bundles on their heads and others in business clothes on their way to office jobs. In that milling early-morning scene, one little boy caught my eye. With his big tray of banana-like plantain fruits on his head, and one finger in his mouth, he was leaning against a shiny Mercedes. He seemed to sum up young Africa, its wealth and poverty, its problems of corruption and political immaturity, in one unspoken word. I took a picture of him, and have since shown it to dozens of audiences for whom it has, I think, captured the point better that I could explain it.

After the short trip across the bay, the coach began its journey through the city, passing first what seemed like mile after mile of derelict shanty shacks. Other people have told me that this upset them deeply, but I quickly realised that what my blue, Caucasian eyes were focusing on was actually a totally different way of life, perfectly adapted, in many ways, to local climatic and economic conditions, and I eventually came to marvel at the efficient survival tactics of these people, their subsistence economy, and their way of supplementing their almost non-existent incomes with home-grown produce, bartering and, if all else failed, recourse to the extended family for support.

Not that these makeshift corrugated-iron hovels in any way represent traditional African dwellings, of course; they are part of the world-wide story of the trek to the city from the rural areas, often in defiance of official persuasion. The favellas of South America and the bustees of Asia are all part of the same theme, and their occupants are, in my view, certainly no more degraded and destitute than are the provincial youths and girls of Europe and America who leave home and lose their identities in the cities, all too often being sucked into vice and drug rings.

The outskirts of the city seemed just like those of any country with a tropical climate, where the stains left by the torrential monsoon rains tend to make even the most attractive buildings take on a shabby, weathered look. Everywhere, one noticed that good buildings stood cheek-by-jowl with the tumbledown shanties, in a way which seems strange to Western eyes, while the wide channels at the sides of the streets bore further witness to the force of the rains.

In the centre of Freetown stands the centuries-old Cotton Tree, the symbol of the city. This magnificent tree, which sheds its leaves seasonally and grows new ones almost overnight, has more character in its massive trunk than many humans have in their faces. It must have been there when the white shippers of the 18th century bought their tragic human merchandise, mostly from the Arab slavers who had been plying the trade for centuries. And that same tree would still be standing to welcome the homecomers and the "recaptives" rescued on the high seas after the shameful traffic had been ended, for it was around this spot that the early settlements of Granville's Town (named after the British philanthropist, Granville Sharp) and Freetown grew up.

I had been booked into the luxurious Bintoumani Hotel, on Lumley Beach, some eight miles from the city centre. In my enthusiasm for my project, I would have preferred to live more "as the Sierra Leoneans do", in less cosmopolitan style, but this taste of hotel life and the transparencies I took there, gave me the opportunity to push the tourist aspect and so, perhaps, promote a little trade.

Within minutes of my arrival, I was being greeted by June, who, in consultation with the Town Hall, had worked out a packed itinerary covering my five precious days — all I could afford as I was paying my own expenses. One of those engagements further enhanced my appreciation of the tourist potential — a fabulous cocktail party at the Mammy Yoko Hotel, outshining any soap opera scenario. Here I met a bewildering array of local and visiting celebrities, ambassadors and tycoons, and sampled Parisian delicacies flown in by a French airline.

The story of Mammy Yoko, the mighty 19th century chieftainess who had once ruled over fifteen chiefdoms, and who, like those other semi-legendary African queens, Dido and Cleopatra, had taken her own life rather than face old age and waning power, is a dramatic one, and would be worth the attention of an enterprising film-maker.

The women of West Africa, it struck me, enjoyed a greater degree of freedom than many other Third World women. Their secret Bundu Society, characterised by curious wooden masks with ringed necks, wielded immense power over a wide area. On my travels, I met many highly-educated and well-qualified women in almost every profession, and, at the most humble level of society, it was pleasing to see small boys working at least as hard as the girls at all; the day-to-day tasks which help the poorer families to survive in these conditions.

At the Town Hall, I was cordially received by Dr Oju Mends, who had succeeded June as Mayor, and by the Town Clerk, Henry Fergusson, and his assistant, Yvette Davies, and was introduced to the City Council's PR officer, Patrick Soji Thomas and to the Mayoral secretary, Gloria Cline-Smythe who was to be my delightful, laughing companion on many of the visits which had been planned for me.

I was taken to a hospital, a private surgery, a children's nursery and a vast covered market crammed with every imaginable object. I spent a morning with fellow journalists at a local newspaper office and visited a school, where I captured some of my best pictures. The children, in their bare, poorly-lit classrooms, seemed so happy, so eager to learn; it made one long to be able to share with them even a fraction of the facilities which so many of our own kids seem to regard as mere vandal-fodder.

On a hill stands the fine, modern Parliament building, where, like all visitors, I was taken to pay my respects at the tomb of Sir Milton Margai, independent Sierra Leone's first Prime Minister. Below, the city lay spread out, beautified by the sunshine and distance, and slightly veiled by the Harmatan, the desert wind which blows a myriad of dust particles along much of the West Coast of Africa. Higher still stands Fourah Bay University, which has an impressive open-air graduation theatre — the only one I have seen to equal it is at the prestigious Vassar College in Poughkeepsie, New York State.

One evening I was invited to meet members of the Ferens Society, made up of graduates of Hull University. The meeting took place at the home of Judge Omrie Golley, and among the guests were several leading members of the Freetown community. It was a relaxed occasion, with a buffet of delicious African dishes organised by Mrs Golley. There was a good deal of serious talk about the efforts being made to implement the principles of justice and democracy in this struggling country, so new in Statehood though old in human experience and culture — but the picture I carried away was one of His Honour jiving to his son's latest pop record, with the rest of us lustily joining in!

I also had opportunities to meet members of the local Rotary, Inner Wheel and Lions' clubs. I believe sincerely in the value of such established and experienced service organisations in promoting international co-operation on a personal level, and at that time I was fortunate in being able to use my newspaper feature to publicise more-or-less systematically the splendid work they do.

One evening, June and her Norwegian husband, Rolv, brought a party of friends to the Bintoumani, where we saw a performance by the colourful and energetic Sierra Leone Dance Company, and afterwards tasted rich delicacies at an African feast, including a concoction of local lobster cooked in a ginger sauce, which I found irresistible.

"The thing about African food is that it looks revolting but tastes delicious," said Rolv. "This is because it is marinated and slow-cooked for hours, and comes out a disgusting dark brown, but oh, the flavour...!" Rolv admitted that whenever he went home to those visually attractive but frankly rather bland-tasting smorgasbords, he could not wait to get back to African cooking. He was also, I discovered, devoted to the Krio language, which seems to bear a similar relationship to English as Yiddish does to High German, and is just as warm and informal. Everyone in Sierra Leone speaks English, which is the first language, although some 12 tribal tongues, including Mende and Temne, are kept alive, but Krio is the true vernacular of the people.

The last evening of my first visit to Freetown is something I shall never forget. Wearing a lovely cotton kaftan — June's gift to me, which I have since worn with pleasure at every possible "Afro" event — I was taken to the local television studio to take part in a gigantic charity-draw organised by the Freetown Lions' Club in aid of a school for blind children. Blindness is a big problem in West Africa, for in addition to trachoma and measles, there is the filaria worm, which infests stagnant water and can get into the eyes and destroy sight. The drive for clean water, for washing as well as for drinking, is therefore paramount, but in the meantime much needs to be done to make life as good as possible for the victims.

During the evening, the children from the school played and sang for us, and I have seldom been so moved in my life. Christmas was fast approaching, and to hear these blind kids giving their version of the Nativity and the joy of welcoming the Christ Child into the world was almost unbearably poignant. African children are never still while they are singing, and their rhythmic movements were infectious — I think everyone in the studio was swaying and rocking by the end of the performance.

Afterwards, I was so emotional that I needed to unwind. June carried me off to a fantastic restaurant right on the beach, and as we sat there drinking coffee under the palm trees, hearing the Atlantic

Ocean whispering its way up the white sand and watching the upside-down tropical crescent moon hanging in the midnight sky, I thought that life could have nothing more magical to offer.

But it had. Suddenly, I became aware that a positive ballet chorus of sand crabs had crept into the strip of light thrown on to the beach from the restaurant. Graceful, translucent little creatures, they danced for us until the lights began to go out and it was time to go.

AN ORGAN FOR WILBERFORCE

By another odd trick of fate, the part of the visit which was to have the greatest on-going effect was not listed on my carefully-prepared itinerary. A series of frantic, and, as it turned out, garbled telephone messages sent me speeding one morning in the Town Hall car to Wilberforce Village, in the hills above the city.

Wilberforce is the name given to a large district which contains some of the finest residential areas in the country, but it is also shared by this small village, and although I was able to spend only a few minutes there, I formed the impression that most of the inhabitants were the direct descendants of one of the original colonies of former slaves who had been the founding fathers of Freetown.

The message I had received was that they wanted me to visit the Methodist Church to see a new organ that was about to be dedicated, but when I arrived and the tangle of wires were uncrossed, it appeared that it was thought I might have news of such an instrument being sent to them from Hull!

What had happened was that when the civic party had come to Freetown the previous year for the twinning ceremonies, the church leaders had approached them to ask whether the people of Hull could be persuaded to help to refurbish the church — the focal point, it seemed, of village society. In particular, they wanted an organ to replace the old, worn-out harmonium which was all they had to accompany the singing. This had put the visiting party in a difficult position, for it had been agreed from the start that friendship, and mutual co-operation on an equal basis, should be the aims of the link, not aid. As I was to learn later, the whole question of aid is an extremely delicate one, needing expert handling. Mistakes are easy to make, and they can be costly in both material and diplomatic terms. I have already mentioned the virtual impossibility of individuals with equal intellectual achievements but widely disparate incomes sharing a really close and active friendship, and the same applies on the larger canvas too.

Nevertheless, when one considered the inequality between the two cities in terms of prosperity, it seemed not unreasonable that, just this once, the citizens of Hull might be disposed to help their fellows in this little African village with the emotive name. The visitors had therefore promised to refer the matter to the Methodist authorities in Hull on their return, to see if they could spearhead some kind of appeal, and this message was duly delivered. Unfortunately, it came through as a simple message of greeting, and nothing was done about it — hence my hosts' anxiety to know how their request had been received.

Even if the request for help had been understood, however, the answer would have had to be a reluctant "no", for three reasons: first the Judea Methodist Church of West Africa is not part of world-wide mainstream Methodism, for this was one of the groups of churches which chose to remain independent when others united in the 1930's. Secondly, the Methodist Church is already fully committed to its own carefully-planned development programme. Thirdly, like most European-based Christian organisations these days, it frowns on expenditure on conventional "churchy" things like organs and vestments, but requires effort to be channelled into practical and educational projects, while worship remains a simple, and essentially "ethnic" thing, based on local culture and resources.

At first, therefore, I received no encouragement at all when I tried to get things moving at the Hull end. This, however, made me more determined than ever that, come what may, by hook or by crook, Wilberforce Methodist Church should have its organ. The "anti's" had all the forces of logic on their side, of course, but I could not forget the forlorn sight of that empty church, which had been cleared for essential structural repairs, while worship was conducted in a small schoolroom nearby; nor could I dismiss the memory of those faces, the simple dignity of those people, their wonderful, shining faith which went back in a direct line to John Wesley, Thomas Coke and the other evangelist-pioneers.

Surely, I argued, they had their priorities right — the greater glory of God. They were prepared quite literally to hunger and thirst after righteousness. They were the meek and the merciful, the pure in heart and the peacemakers, the great-great-grandsons and daughters of the persecuted, and surely they were blessed.

Some of the objections I heard from self-styled Christians made me quite angry. Missionaries used to speak of "Rice Christians", who would embrace the faith to secure their daily handout. Now, it seemed to me, we Europeans were the "Rice Christians", having to be wooed to church with youth clubs and rock music and old folks' leisure days and anything and everything except basic worship, while far away, under that upside-down crescent moon, my friends in Wilberforce were getting it right. What did it matter if their conception of Christian worship was "that of an English Methodist Church 100 years ago"? Chapels were full in those days, in the Welsh valleys and the Yorkshire Dales. Now, most of them have been pulled down or turned into weekend cottages or filling-stations. Wilberforce Church could muster a choir of 40 *men* — more than one would find in many an entire congregation here.

One thing, however, was clear from the start. It would be no use trying to obtain and send out any kind of conventional pipe organ, which would become a wreck in no time, due to the tropical damp and the termites. A modern electronic organ, on the other hand, would stand a reasonable chance of giving good service for many years, besides being compact and easier to transport. It so happened that during the next few months there appeared to be a cash-flow problem in the electronic organ market, and numerous "bargains" were offered in the shops and through the media. An idea was taking shape in my mind...but no — I'd never get away with it!

One Sunday, however, I was on an outing with the Soroptimist Club, and our first stop was at Malton. As we drew up in the market place, I saw a large pantechnicon unloading at the hall opposite, and went to investigate. It was, of all incongruous things to find on a Sunday afternoon in a charming Yorkshire market town, a display of electronic organs, backing a big sales drive. If ever I received a "sign from heaven", this was surely it!

It was no use hanging about. Action had to be swift if we were not to miss out on the bonanza of special offers. I invented an "anonymous well-wisher" willing to put up the money, talked the Freetown Society into backing the scheme, and launched an appeal through my newspaper column. City Organist Peter Goodman lent his expertise in selecting a suitable instrument — an Italian Farfisa which, despite its relatively small size and modest price, was capable of everything from a full-throated ecclesiastical blast to a toe-tickling Caribbean rhythm, making it a versatile asset to the village community for recreational purposes as well as for worship. It was bought and stored in a convenient corner of the City Hall until we could find ways and means of sending it out.

At last I was no longer battling alone. The idea caught on and imaginations were stirred. My Soroptimist sisters gave superb support, collaborating with the Freetown Society to put on a concert. Armed with a tape illustrating the organ's capabilities, I gave talks at churches and clubs, which weighed in with donations, and in no time at all we had received more than enough to repay that "anonymous well-wisher" and cover the transport costs as well. As it happened, we did not need to use the balance for that purpose, for, through the influence of the Council-based Freetown Society, a local industrialist volunteered to have the organ crated and sent to London docks, where a shipping line had agreed to transport it to Freetown free of charge. The extra money could therefore be channelled into an educational fund — a comforter for those who were probably still doubtful about the wisdom of sending the organ.

Meantime, I was still concerned about the enormous cost of replacing the Wilberforce Church's worn-out hymn-books. Luck, however, was once again on my side, for the British Methodist Church was just about to issue an up-dated edition, and it seemed likely that some of the old ones, still in good condition, would become available. Again I appealed through the column — and nagged Methodist friends — and received more than 50 copies of the words-only books plus 20 with the music as well, all in excellent condition. These were duly boxed up and sent out through the good offices of the Guildhall.

I well remember going to Beverley to pick up the music books. The pedestrian precincts and one-way systems in that beautiful old town defy description, but, following the explicit instructions of the kindly choir-mistress, I finally arrived in a supermarket car-park at the back of the church.

"We shall have to climb over the wall," said she, explaining that there had been a fire at the church a few days before, and the appropriate entrance was unsafe and had needed to be blocked off. So the astonished supermarket staff and customers were treated to the spectacle of two middle-aged ladies in tight skirts repeatedly scrambling over a four-foot wall with as much decorum as they could muster, carrying boxes and armfuls of books and sheet music and stuffing them into the car boot.

The friendships formed through this church project were, of course, enduring, and when I revisited Freetown in 1987 as a member of the civic delegation attending the Bicentenary celebrations of the founding of the colony, I was made an honorary member of the congregation in a simple but unforgettable ceremony.

For the record, I should perhaps also say that by this time the system in Freetown had changed, and the city was being run by a Committee of Management under the chairmanship of Mr Alfred Akibo-Betts, while, to our great delight, Gloria Cline-Smythe had become acting Town Clerk.

However, another adventure was in my pipeline as the bells rang in the New Year of 1982.

ISRAEL UNDER FIRE

For some time, I had been planning to visit a correspondent of long standing, Hull-born journalist Annette Goodman, who had "made aliya" - a Hebrew word which literally means "going up" - to Israel some years before we started writing to each other. Annette had settled in a township near Haifa, and I knew that she would be able to put me in touch with other Hull people who had also "gone up", giving further scope for articles and talks which would be of interest to people back home. That, to begin with, was my whole intent.

However, in the summer of 1982 came Israel's controversial entry into Southern Lebanon, to clear an area which they claimed had become a launch-pad for terrorist raids on their Galilean towns and settlements. This operation culminated in the much-publicised massacres by unidentified Lebanese militia of Palestinians in refugee camps at Sabra and Chatilla. These massacres were, in fact, no worse than many which had taken place during the long period of multi-faction chaos which had beset the lovely land of Lebanon, once the affluent Switzerland of the Middle East and now in political tatters. But as Israeli forces were controlling the area at the time, most of the blame fell on them and they were savagely attacked in the world's media.

My impending visit therefore took on a greater significance. What was life like in Israel now that this small but vitally important democracy, with its powerful Western allies, found itself in such a delicate position diplomatically? How was it affecting the life of the people in the streets of Jerusalem and Tel-Aviv?

During my years of social isolation and personal problems, I had drawn great comfort from the friendship of Jewish people, who, with their unique experience of human tragedy, seem to have a true understanding of loneliness and sorrow. Their combination of warmth, personality and brightness of intellect had fed a deep need in me, and I felt I owed them a great deal. Already, in 1963, I had made a brief visit to the relatively new and raw Jewish State, and, of course, had written about its pioneering zeal with great enthusiasm.

I had joined the York Anglo-Israel Friendship Society, which was then the nearest branch, and, with the help of the secretary, the late Benny Brent, and the World Zionist Organisation in Jerusalem, a rather special itinerary was planned for my 1982 visit. Benny also linked me up with a delightful travelling companion, Councillor Mrs Dorothy Clegg, later Mayor of Whitby, and we were to become firm friends.

I had also made the acquaintance of Israeli journalist Ofra Yeshua Lyth, a news editor at *"Maariv"*, the leading Hebrew language newspaper, and she had promised me some special contacts too. I had got to know Ofra when her English husband, Peter, was completing a project at Hull University.

Getting to Israel in October 1982 was no easy matter, for the El Al airline was strike-bound, but after long delays, Dorothy and I eventually found ourselves airborne in a chartered Malaysian jet. Peter and Ofra met us at Ben Gurion airport, and never had we been so pleased to see friendly faces, for we were both exhausted — Dorothy was incubating 'flu — and we had no idea how we were going to get to Haifa. They put us on the right bus, and, despite our fatigue, we were overwhelmed by the beauty of the city by night, seen from our hotel halfway up Mount Carmel. It is a curious fact, I think, that unless you know Israel really well, you forget how small the country is, and how easy it is to get around by bus!

Next morning there was an emotional meeting with Annette, who took Dorothy and myself by bus to Nahariya, on the northern coast, where we had lunch with Manchester-born author and journalist Hadassa Bat Haim. Lunch with an Israeli housewife is a memorable experience, for the food is excellent and plentiful, and is served without fuss or formality. The big pot of succulent pasta and meat sauce was set on the table, and we could come back for "seconds" and even "thirds". There is always salad — huge tomatoes, sliced cucumbers, fresh and pickled, and, of course, luscious fruits, although, in their zeal to export the best, Israelis sometimes find themselves left with the rejects. Lunching later on a kibbutz, I caused hearty laughter when I peeled an orange and discovered it to be black and squelchy inside.

Hadassa showed us round the town, pointing out the spots where shells had been lobbed over from Lebanon, and the house whose occupants had been wiped out during a raid in which the terrorists had tried to storm the school and take the children hostage. Nahariya was also the scene of a different kind of "shooting", when the film *Judith* was made there, bringing not only a little pleasurable excitement for a change but some financial benefit to the town also. A new bridge was constructed with the proceeds and named after the star of the film — Sophia Loren!

We drove north to Rosh Hanikra, on the border with Lebanon, ostensibly to see the famous water-caves which are at least as spectacular as Italy's Blue Grotto; but inevitably our attention focused on the cross-border traffic. White UNIFIL vehicles were everywhere, together with the brown service trucks and the Magan David Adom ambulances — Israel's "Red Star", which treats friend and foe alike.

Newsreels invariably show Israel's fighting men as bronzed, rather arrogant-looking professional soldiers, armed to the teeth with all the latest weaponry, and, indeed, the country has its crack units of the calibre which rescued the hijack hostages from Entebbe. But I think one must go to Israel and mingle with the people to appreciate the true picture; the Israeli Defence Force is essentially a civilian army of reservists — Chaim's son and Rachael's brother and little Yitzak's dad — that is how they are regarded at home and the impression is anything but grimly militaristic.

In that scene on the border, soldier and civilian exchanged greetings and conversation in the most casual way. There were few foreign tourists about, apart from ourselves — the industry, vital to Israel's economy, had taken a knock that year — but many nationals were on holiday, including children and young people, and they made an incongruous but strangely touching sight in their shorts and summer gear against that stark frontier backcloth.

It was the Feast of Succoth, Harvest Thanksgiving, when Jewish families make little tabernacles in their yards and gardens, eating, and even sleeping in them during the festival, which the children, in particular, enjoy. We saw an elderly Jew, heavily bearded and in black, hand to one of the young soldiers a "lulav", a harvest symbol made of four branches, citrus, myrtle, palm and pomegranate. This was only one of many little incidents we saw during our visit which seemed to telescope the centuries, underlining the deep, deep roots the Children of Israel have put down in this land since their ancestor, Abraham, and his companions arrived there some 4,000 years ago to set up as peaceful settlers, sharing the resources with the other tribes they found there.

The more I consider this vexed question of territorial rights, the more I feel that these can no longer be automatically linked to ethnic origins. Anthropologists today appear to favour the theory that the human species originated in only a few parts of the world, and, over the succeeding millennia, spread to the other areas of the earth by migration. Even the American Indians are now thought to have come from Asia, trekking through Alaska when the two continents were joined, and moving southward and eastward. If the New Zealand Maoris succeed in wresting "their" land back from the white Pakeha, will they then hand it over in turn to the descendants of the original islanders from whom they took it when they arrived in their Kon Tiki rafts? And were those islanders, in truth, the original inhabitants, or did they, in their turn, conquer, annihilate or integrate with even earlier residents?

So it is the world over. We are so mixed up and inter-related now that the best we can do, as a human race, is to try to allocate land in the best possible way to create as much peace and justice as we can — bearing in mind that one person's human rights is another's oppression and occupation. Nowhere is this more starkly represented than in the Middle East, but when I came to write about my experiences later, what upset and angered me most was the sheer ignorance of many of my anti-Zionist opponents. They were unaware, for instance, that the Palestinians were given their own State — Jordan — in 1922, and that the Jews had had to wait another 35 years, and lose six million people in the Holocaust before being given a tiny sliver of the land they had been promised as far back as 1917.

Not one hectare of land was snatched from Arab owners. All was bought fairly and squarely — but unfortunately, many of the owners were absentee landlords, and the land was occupied by poor, illiterate tenants who had no idea of what was going on. Even in stable, developed countries like Britain, it is impossible to build a road, clear a slum or construct a reservoir to provide clean water for thousands of people without having to drag some little old lady kicking and screaming out of the hovel she has occupied all her life. Multiply this by thousands, and you have some idea of the problems facing the new State of Israel, problems exacerbated by the fact that, as the early pioneers had gradually succeeded, through sheer hard work and the intelligent application of knowledge, in clearing the malarial swamps and reclaiming the neglected land, the non-Jewish population had also grown by leaps and bounds, attracted by the rising standard of living.

By my reckoning, therefore, no one had an automatic right, on purely ethnic grounds, to that much-disputed land. But once to every man and nation, it seems, comes a moment when some united voice from the inmost depths of their being, cries, "This is the place!" It happened to Brigham Young and his Mormon pioneers when, on July 24, 1847, they first clapped eyes on the Salt Lake Valley. It probably happened to those red-skinned Asians when they saw the prairies and forests of North America, and to the Maori raft-paddlers when they glimpsed the shores of the Land of the Long White Cloud. And it had certainly happened to Abraham when he reached the Land of Canaan, and to Moses when, after the long sojourn in Egypt and the years of nomadic existence in the desert, he viewed the same stretch of country from afar.

Home, in short, is where you feel at home. When I visited my grandmother's native city of Venice, it struck me as being wet, smelly and claustrophobic. I like Scotland, where some of my other ancestors came from, but have no particular wish to live there. On the other hand, I have felt warm surges of happiness in a number of the countries I have visited, even though I have no ethnic or cultural link with them. In an ideal world, we would all be able to live where we liked, but as things are, this is not always possible and we must do the best we can.

Millions of Jewish people have settled "in the diaspora", but it is vitally necessary that they should have a country of their own, particularly in view of the ever-present menace of antisemitism, which, even as I write, is heaving its slimy presence out of the swamp in Western and Central Europe, as well as in Russia, where is has never died; even in our own country, it is just below the surface. And for the Jew, Israel is indisputably "the place".

From Rosh Hanikra, Dorothy and I journeyed by bus with Annette to Acre, or Akko, the old Crusader port which is a mecca for tourists, and was en fete for Succoth, with carnival characters and stilt-walkers all jigging to the latest Western pop tunes.

Next day, Dorothy's 'flu got the better of her, so she stayed in the hotel, enjoying the sunshine and the wonderful view while I accompanied Annette to Kibbutz Amiad, a Galilean settlement where her nephew, Geoffrey Goodman, had come to live with his Manchester-born wife, Susan, and their three children, Chana, who had recently been married, son Giora and eleven-year old Debbie.

Israel today embraces many lifestyles, from the total withdrawal from the 20th century practised by the extreme religious sects, who will not even recognise the State "until Messiah comes" to completely free enterprise. But here, on the kibbutz, one finds the same idealism which made the modern miracle of Israel possible. In 1982, for instance, Amiad was being managed by Dr Echud Artsi, a world authority on body-scanners — and he was receiving the same pocket-money allowance as the other one hundred and eighty members.

In 1946, water had to be brought daily to the settlement by donkey cart from Rosh Pina, and the settlers were employed in stone-clearing and afforestation — when they were not on guard duty. Today, Amiad is a highly-mechanised, fully computerised unit. After an excellent lunch in the communal dining room, I offered to help with the washing-up thinking that this was the done thing in this egalitarian society. My hosts smiled indulgently and ushered me to a large utility room equipped with an industrial dish-washer. "You can put your knife and fork on the conveyor-belt if you like. There! Now you can say you have washed up on a kibbutz!" I picked a couple of avocados, too, for good measure as we toured the estate.

Amiad, which is fairly typical of the medium-sized, well-established kibbutz, has a mixed economy. At its heart is a factory where some of the most up-to-date filters are made for industry and agriculture. I saw one which had just come off the drawing-board and was quite revolutionary. The factory, Geoffrey told me, provided the last link in the system affording a full life for the women of the community. Previously, when their child-rearing days were over, they had no alternative to agricultural work, which did not suit all of them. Now, the factory provides another option, and the lighter jobs enable older or less fit members to be useful.

The factory provides 50 per cent of the kibbutz economy, while the remainder comes from a beef herd of 800 animals, 40,000 head of poultry — Geoffrey later obtained a degree in poultry management at the Hebrew University — and plantations of bananas, cotton, kiwi-fruits, oranges, grapefruit and avocados scattered around the Galilee.

It was Debbie Goodman who showed me round the children's

farm, run by the young kibbutzniks with just a little adult help. This is much more than a play-farm, though the children do get a lot of fun out of it, and besides the sheep and poultry kept for commercial purposes, I saw a number of pets.

I was brought down from this innocent pastorale with a bump when I was taken into the deep shelter, equipped to deal with everything from gas ("We never know what they are going to throw at us next") to nuclear fall-out. With one hundred and eighty members and candidates, about one hundred and ten children and anything between forty and seventy young volunteer workers to care for at any one time, security has a big priority.

Kibbutz life is not so "communal" as it used to be, I discovered. Families have their own homes with separate amenities and pleasant small gardens. Children can now sleep in the parental home, though they spend most of the day in communal quarters when they are not in school. Kibbutz parents, however, are never far away, and can pop in and see their young ones more frequently than can working parents in conventional societies.

As we waited for the bus beside the busy road linking the Lebanese border with Central Israel, and while Geoffrey was trying to teach me to count in Hebrew, I reflected that there had been many people in the early days who wondered whether the kibbutzim, moshavim, co-operatives and other experimental communities would survive the growing affluence and viability of the developing State. Would human avarice take over from the principle of "to each according to his need!"? It was reassuring to meet so many who were still willing to deny the Great God Differential and find fulfilment in this way of life.

JOY AMID THE DANGER

Haifa may not be so majestically historic as Jerusalem or so earthy and entertaining as Tel-Aviv, but it is still one of the loveliest cities I know, and while there I spent some time at the beautiful golden Shrine of the Bab, the headquarters of the Baha'i Faith. Many tourists think that this shrine, in its quiet, formal garden, houses the bones of the founder of the faith, the 19th century Persian prophet Husayn Ali, known as Baha'u'llah, "The Glory of God", but it is in fact the resting-place of the young John the Baptist style visionary, Siyyid Ali-Muhammad, who preceded him and foretold his coming, and who was executed by a firing squad in Tabriz at the age of thirty-one, when the authorities, believing the new religion to be dangerously heretical, were trying to stamp it out. The shrine of Baha'u'llah, who himself suffered many years of imprisonment, is at Bahji, just north of Acre.

I have many friends among the Baha'i community in Humberside, and have long admired their gentle way of life and uncomplicated belief in the essential unity to be found in the diversity of all created things, their acceptance of scientific discovery in the confidence that all can be used for good, and their insistence on the equal value of the sexes. So it was a particular pleasure to see this exquisite place once again and savour its peaceful and hopeful atmosphere.

From Haifa, Dorothy and I moved on to Tiberias, on the shores of Lake Kinneret, the harp-shaped Sea of Galilee. We did not care much for the town itself, finding it rather dirty, with open rubbish-skips and a multitude of stray cats foraging among them. Up to the time of the Six Day War in 1967, it was impossible to develop the place properly because of its vulnerability to attack from the Golan Heights, and since that time, of course, there have been other priorities, but we did see new hotels being built and efforts being made to improve the amenities and promote the use of the thermal springs which tempted the Romans to establish a town there in the first place.

We were lucky enough to be booked in at the Church of Scotland Hospice, an inexpensive oasis of scrupulous cleanliness and tranquil beauty amid the heat and litter. There, we met a fascinating collection of people, and spent a wonderful evening exchanging national songs and dances with a group of the liveliest nuns I have ever come across. They were staying at the convent next door, and represented many lands, including Korea, Kenya, Zambia, India and Thailand. "Off duty", if there is such a thing for nuns, they were allowed to wear their national dress, and very colourful they looked.

Tiberias is famous for its lakeside cafes, with their wonderful views of the salmon-pink Golan Heights rising from the water on the far side. Here you can enjoy the local St. Peter's Fish — even the Israelis call them that! — with chips and rounds of pitta bread, and the cats will finish the leftovers for you. Why does fish always taste better in the open air?

From Tiberias we took the bus to Jerusalem, passing through the disputed West Bank in a journey I shall never forget. Every time you take a journey on an Israeli service bus in the 1980's you feel like part of a film set. There are the weary young soldiers, dropping asleep in the heat, yet never relaxing their grip on their guns. There are the tidy housewives with their Polish style hair or headscarves, the children with their cans of CocaCola, the inevitable parchment-faced Chassid, with his black hat and side-curls, and, in contrast, the sun-tanned kibbutznik in his shorts and open-necked shirt.

The bus seemed to be going like the clappers through the cinnamon-coloured landscape, the Arab villages flashing past in a blur like giant egg-boxes. "Is he afraid we are going to be ambushed?" I nervously inquired of the kibbutznik, with whom I had got into conversation. He smiled: "No," he replied in confident American-English, "They always drive like this — some go faster!"

The driver must have become thirsty, however, because we stopped at a wayside refreshment stall, and as we gulped our drinks, I took what proved to be one of my evocative pictures. It shows the ever-vigilant soldiers on guard while a young couple on a seat gaze into each other's eyes over their icecream cornets. Time for romance, time for living, time for joy amid all the tension and danger.

In the bus again, we sped through the outskirts of Jericho, the world's oldest known city, and then began the long, twisting ascent through the hills to Jerusalem, the route taken, in reverse, by the Good Samaritan and his protege so long ago, and could be the scene of a repeat performance any minute, I feared, as the terrain was just as perfect for terrorist attack as it must have been 2,000 years before.

If we did not "fall among thieves" on our way from Jericho to Jerusalem, that omission was soon righted when we got there! The first was a taxi-driver who took us to the wrong gate of the Old City and charged us seventy shekels for the privilege. There, several porters fell upon our luggage, squabbling among themselves as to who was to transport it, the winner loading it upon a handcart and setting off at a brisk pace through the narrow, crowded streets with the two of us trying to keep up. Both of us were limping, as I had a huge, painful mosquito bite on my leg and Dorothy had lost the heel of her sandal.

We had told the porter that we wanted to be at the Hospice of the Sisters of Zion, which we knew to be in the Via Dolorosa, but apparently the only word he vaguely understood was "Hospice", and after about 10 minutes of stumbling over the rough, stepped alley-ways, being jostled by the stall-holders and their customers, children and donkeys, we were ushered into a large courtyard which was obviously not where we should have arrived. "Hospice!" said the porter proudly, and held out his hand for payment. A hospice it certainly was, but not that of the Sisters of Zion. It was clear that the porter did not know where that was, and that it was useless trying to explain, so we offered him a very fair price for his labours and decided to ask for directions from the people sitting in the courtyard.

The porter was not satisfied. He wanted more money and started to argue, probably thinking that two English ladies would be easily intimidated. But he had reckoned without that formidable force, the British woman town councillor. Dorothy, with a mein that had caused many a fractious local government committee member to tremble, stood up to him, holding her own until some young Australians who had been watching the proceedings, came across, dismissed the disgruntled porter with a few more shekels and a couple of choice Aussie cuss-words, and then - bless their hearts - picked up our bags and led us once more through the teeming souk to our destination, vanishing into the crowd before we could even thank them properly.

The Hospice, set in just about the most poignant site in Christendom, is a weird place, awesome and even frightening, but staying there was an experience I would not have missed. It is built over the best-authenticated relic of the life and times of Christ yet discovered — the site of Pontius Pilate's fortress, where he would judge cases brought before him, and in the crypt stands part of a column which, it is said, Jesus would actually have passed four times on his last day on earth. During our stay, we "did" many of the obligatory sites connected with the New Testament history, including the little Arab town of Bethlehem, which we found less debased than we had feared, despite its plethora of souvenir shops, but none of those sites, so far as we could gather, carried the same degree of authenticity in that much-destroyed and rebuilt city.

Photographers frequently call at the Hospice and ask to be allowed on to the roof terrace, from where an unsurpassed view can be seen over the gold and silver Muslim domes, the Christian shrines and other historic buildings of Old Jerusalem. We had free access to this superb scene throughout our stay, and took full advantage of it.

Every morning, in our rather austere quarters, we were awakened at five by the grotesquely amplified sound of the Muezzin calling the faithful to prayer from the many mosques; but we were rewarded by the sight of pretty, well-dressed Arab children making their way to school through the streets below, a reminder that the communities can, and do, live side by side in harmony and prosperity.

During our few precious Jerusalem days, we toured that matchless city from Western Wall to Knesset parliament, saw the legendary Mayor, Teddy Kollek, wrestling with the ultra-orthodox awkward squad at a city council meeting, shopped at the WIZO charity store in the Jaffa Road, with its array of beautiful handcrafted goods — and took a bus to the outskirts to plant some trees in the afforestation scheme.

The bus driver was most helpful, especially as we were running late, and made it only just before closing time. I have a feeling he went off his normal route to drop us at the right point, where the road fell away into a steep, stony track leading down to the plantation. Wearing our best dresses and shoes, for we had both had interviews with VIP's that morning, I at the Christian Embassy and Dorothy with a city council official, we flew down the road.

At the bottom of the hill, beside a small hut, we saw a little man obviously making preparations to leave. We waved and called to him and he halted. Like most English tourists, I harbour the unshakable belief that if you speak very loudly and clearly in your own language, any foreigner can understand you. As we approached, I panted, "We've come — all the way — from England — to plant — some trees!" Adjusting his yarmulka, the little man smiled. "Have ye, begorra?" he replied. "Sure, and I've come all the way from Belfast meself!" That's Israel for you!

As I knelt on that rough, stony Judean hillside planting my tiny fir tree, helped by that little Irish Jew, I felt strangely at one with all the prophets and kings, the pioneers and visionaries, the millions of ordinary folk who had passed that way before me. Oh, why should a White Anglo-Saxon Protestant — well, part Celt, part Latin, part Heaven-knows-what sceptic — feel this Ruth-like affinity with Israel? I can only think that, no matter how cynical or "lapsed" we may be, our Christian conditioning goes deeper than we think, and this is our spiritual home, whether our logical conscious mind recognises it or not.

From Jerusalem, we were taken to the Dead Sea area, where we ascended the great rock-fortress of Masada, the scene of the rebels' last stand against the occupying Romans in the AD70's, ending in their choice of mass suicide rather than capture. I would have preferred to walk up, but as it was an exceptionally hot day for October, and I think our guides had visions of some of us freaking out with sunstroke, we were ushered into the cable car. Our guide proved to be exceptionally skilful in conjuring up on that burning heap of rock and rubble the fantastic palace built by Herod the Great, with its amazing resources of food and water which enabled the besieged to hold out so long against their parched, sun-scorched besiegers.

Soon we were back in the twentieth century — or were we? The incredible Dead Sea Works, which were next on our itinerary, have an uncanny tie-up with the 2,500-year-old prophecies of Ezekiel, who had a strange vision of water coming eastward across the desert sands, sweetening the dead lake and making it teem with fish and the surrounding land with good things — Chapter 47, if you want to look it up. The scheme, according to Schlomo Drori, who explained it to us with more-than-Yiddisher enthusiasm and gesture, was actually envisaged back in the nineteenth century by Theodor Herzl, the founder of modern Zionism, who suggested cutting a canal from the Mediterranean to the Dead Sea. This has now been translated on the drawing-board into a tunnel from the Gaza coast through the

Judean hills. It would, we were told, be the deepest tunnel in the world, and would bring just sufficient water to the rapidly-shrinking inland sea to keep it topped up. The sea has been silting up since its fresh feed-water from Lake Kinneret and the Jordan had been tapped to irrigate the Negev Desert.

When the water from the tunnel reached the 1,200 foot drop to the Rift, said Schlomo, its force could be used to turn huge turbines, creating hydro-electric power. But this was nothing to the massive sources of energy which would then be created by turning the Dead Sea into a gigantic solar pond!

Already, by 1982, a dyke had been built along the length of the sea. This, Schlomo told us, was begun by a team of American engineers who successfully completed the part where the bed-salt was one metre thick, but gave up when it reached three metres. Dutch experts were consulted. They examined the problem and then pronounced, "We cannot do it. You will have to do it yourselves!" "But you are the world's experts on dykes — how come you cannot do it and we can?" queried the Israelis. "You have no option!" was the dry response. And they did it.

"It is up to us to do it," Schlomo told us with prophetic zeal. "We Israelis have not only the technology but the morality. The Dead Sea Works are the biggest enterprise in the world based on solar energy. We have the raw materials to supply world consumption for years to come, and we don't need oil to work it, we need cheap electricity."

"The only real hope of peace in the Middle East is co-operation based on what Israel can give. Jordan is building the most modern potash industry, but it will not work because they don't have the know-how. We do. The future of Israel is in this area. The State of Israel will become an inspiration for the whole world. The whole world can co-operate if one nation can give to the other. The essence of Judaism is giving — the real strength of a country is not what it can take but what it can give."

Thanks to my retained ability to write fairly rapid shorthand, I got all this down, and, as we thanked Schlomo and promised to do all we could to spread the word that "From the Sea of Death comes Life", I rummaged in my purse and found a souvenir pencil giving dimensions of the Humber Bridge. I handed it to him: "'They said we couldn't do it either," I told him.

WHERE 'CHEN' MEANS 'CHARM'

There is a World War I story which tells how the Prince of Wales, later briefly King Edward VIII, pleaded to be allowed to take part in active service, saying, "It would not be such a catastrophe if I were killed." "It is not that which worries me, Sir", replied the commander, "But it would be a different matter if you were taken prisoner!"

The same applies to Israel's girl soldiers. Except for certain key personnel, they are not allowed near the fighting lines — but they do practically everything else, and the country's stretched military resources would be in a bad way without them.

Through Ofra's influence, I obtained a temporary Israeli Press Pass, and this got me into the camp, "somewhere near Tel Aviv", where she had herself completed her Army training. The officers, male and female, seemed none too pleased to see me at first - British journalists were not exactly the flavour of the month just then, and I could sense that I was being very closely watched. I had to work hard to win them over, but by the end of the afternoon things had relaxed. I was wearing replicas of the IDF badge — a sword in an olive branch, symbolising Israel's desire for peace — and of the unit badge, and I had been photographed cuddling an UZI sub-machine gun!

CHEN is the Hebrew acronym for the Women's Corps, and appropriately it is also the word for "charm". But these beautiful, sun-tanned girls in their designer uniforms are not just pretty faces. Every able-bodied single girl is called up for military service at sixteen, and although the ultra-orthodox can obtain exemption, many volunteer for some form of non-military service. National service is the gateway to further education for many girls, especially those who have missed out earlier in life, and about two hundred courses are available to them, covering everything from office and administrative jobs to high technology.

As entry standards are higher for girls than for men, it sometimes happens, as in the camp I visited, that the girls find themselves being waited on by men, who do the cooking and general chores while the girls are occupied on complex courses — but I was told that there was no ill-feeling. Over a cup of coffee and a piece of IDF cake, made by the men cooks, the Lieutenant Colonel in charge of the unit, a pleasant, thirty-four year-old woman with a family, told me that while the discipline inside the camp was necessarily tight, officers and girls enjoyed friendly informal relationships when they were off duty. Despite the conveyor-belt efficiency which had to be maintained in processing endless batches of recruits into soldiers, every effort was made to keep the face of the Army human. I saw, for instance, little plots of flowers planted by the girls around their rather Spartan huts, a characteristically feminine touch, softening the harsh, military background.

I formed the impression that Israeli women were not fiercely feminist. They are too proud of their roles as wives and mothers to put careers before family life — indeed, some are honest enough to remain single rather than do half a job. But Israel seems to have gone further than any other country I know in finding ways of using its manpower and womanpower to the best advantage without coercion.

Ofra also managed to fix an interview for me with Major Irit Atsmon — her name means "Flower of the Mountain". Irit was the IDF's liaison officer for the foreign Press, and had earlier handled Press relations during the visits of President Jimmy Carter of the United States and President Sadat of Egypt. Our meeting was to have been a formal briefing on the military situation, but as we sat in her office, with huge maps on the walls and a pile of explanatory literature before us, it somehow did not work out like that.

I suppose it is my early brushes with classic literature that so often make me aware of touches of drama in real-life situations. There we sat, two women from two different worlds, brought together for a brief moment by the most unlikely set of circumstances, one life shaped and dominated by the huge, horrific, shared nightmare of the Holocaust, the other by comparison so sheltered and protected from physical harm, yet having had to claw its way towards the light through intangible barriers erected long ago by adverse demographic factors and by the fears and phobias of others.

"Last time I was in Beirut, I suddenly felt tired...so tired", I heard the small, pretty woman on the other side of the desk saying wearily.

"Does the rest of the world think we like killing and hurting people, after all we have been through ourselves? When we see children crying in Beirut, we cry too. When I see old people homeless, hurt and bewildered, I think of my own people...I think of my mother and all that she endured. I was born here of a disaster-family, but we were never taught to hate our enemies."

"All we want to do is to preserve our democracy and our values. The IDF is the face of the nation — our Army is mostly made up of reservists. Israel does not want to stay in Lebanon once all foreign forces are out, including the Syrians."

Israelis in general, I found, were hurt and bewildered by the reaction of the world's media to their activities in Lebanon. But Irit was not surprised by the criticism: "It is the same in a family. When the baby is small, everybody pets it and make a fuss of it, but when the child begins to grow into an adult and to act independently, the grown-ups say this is *chutzpah* — audacity. When we were a young, struggling nation, we received a lot of sympathy and support. Now we are beginning to stand on our feet it is different."

When I started writing this account, I hoped to make it non-partisan, but that is proving impossible! My affection for Israel and the Israelis was, however, shared wholeheartedly by some British nuns I met at the Hospice in Jerusalem. They had been working at an 800-pupil school run by their Order in East Beirut and were on leave in Jerusalem while the building was being repaired after a bomb attack.

"We do not know who dropped the bombs, but we are certain it was not the Israelis," said one of the Sisters, who went on to give me, as far as she could, a run-down on the hideously complicated political happenings which had led to the chaos in Lebanon.

It was a matter of sorrow to the Sisters that Western Christians seemed to have abandoned their brethren in that country. The idea, widespread in Europe, that "Christian" was a mere political label, and that the Maronites were an archaic splinter sect constituting just another quarrelsome faction, was totally false, they told me. The Maronites are descendants of the early converts made by St Paul in the First Century, and they take their name from St Maron, who "civilised" the area in the Middle Ages. They are devout, practising Christians, said the Sister, and when the Palestine Liberation Organisation, having been turned out of Jordan, first entered Lebanon, the community offered them hospitality. Eventually, however, both Muslim and Christian Lebanese were anxious to be rid of the PLO. It was now essential that "a multi-nation force should police the country until a new government was established."

One of the Sisters told me that she knew the ruling Gemayal family personally. The father, Pierre, was "a good man whose home was as simple as a priest's cell." His son, Bashir, who had recently been assassinated, had been "a martyr to the cause of peace". He had known that his life would be in danger when he accepted the presidency, but it had been hoped that he would live for at least a year. When Bashir (who was, of course, succeeded by his brother, Amin) was killed, it was said of him "Never in the history of Lebanon, ancient or modern, had there been a man who caused so many dreams to be born and whose death caused so many tears to fall."

As soon as the news of the assassination broke, said Sister, all the younger Lebanese soldiers were immediately confined to barracks and the older ones disarmed to try and prevent reprisals from taking place, so she believed it could not have been any of the main units which carried out the Sabra and Chatilla massacres. Her guess was that a small band of attackers was led by "some who were sick in mind after having experienced the same things being done to their own families."

Even members of religious orders, dedicated to the truth and with no axes to grind, political or commercial, can have prejudices, or be mistaken or misinformed, but these intelligent, mature women obviously believed every word of what they were saying — and, of course, our chance meeting provided me with some superb, and highly topical copy.

Israel is, in fact, in many ways a journalist's paradise. You don't have to interview people — they tell you their life-stories without being asked:

"I was in Auschwitz *and* Buchenwald", vouchsafed the taxi-driver taking me to the Press headquarters in Tel-Aviv one day. "Then, when I got here, the British wanted to hang me because I had a gun — a little gun, to defend myself from the Arabs! OK, I told them, OK — go ahead, hang me and finish the job. My father and mother and six brothers and sisters are all dead; so now you finish the job — wipe out the whole family. So in the end they let me go."

The British, in fact, have a bad image in museums commemorating the postwar immigration saga, and we had to keep reminding people that we had fought Hitler and Mussolini for six long years, and had stopped Rommel from sweeping across North Africa, that we had had a difficult job to do and that uncontrolled immigration always brings trouble, no matter how sympathetic one might be to the would-be immigrants or how desperate their need.

This lack of understanding of Britain's hellishly difficult situation during those years was the one thing which struck a slightly jarring note. But I could not remain at cross purposes with this unique land for very long, and as Dorothy and I boarded the chartered British Midlands plane — twenty-four hours late because of the on-going strike — to fly back to Heathrow, I knew I was going to miss those wonderful mornings, with the scent of jasmine and rosemary and the sight of tall cyprus trees etched against the hard, blue sky and a big, brown military helicopter clacking by. I was going to miss falling over history in the street, mesmeric music in the minor key, and food which, despite all those complicated dietory laws, was always interesting and flavourful. Above all, I was going to miss that incredible mixture of people.

The articles and slide-shows I produced on my return naturally caused some controversy, but they were equally understandably well received by Jewish communities in Britain, the USA and Israel itself, and today one wall of my room is embellished with certificates recording the planting of trees in my name in Israel's soil — the most touching gift anyone could receive.

All I can say is that I tried as far as I could to record my impressions sincerely, and one of the themes I tried to highlight was summed up in a quote from one of our guides: "There can be no peace for us, physically or spiritually, until there is peace for the Palestinian refugees."

AN AMBITION FULFILLED

These sagas of mine may seem tame when compared with the adventurous projects, often of much longer duration, which are almost routine for many young people these days, or with dangerous investigative assignments undertaken by national media journalists. But it must be remembered that mine were not official assignments — they were completely one-off affairs, for which I received no financial sponsorship or official backing from any source whatsoever.

Moreover, I was now in my late fifty's, but, strangely enough, I felt physically fitter and mentally more confident than I had ever done in my life. It is too seldom recognised, I believe, that many women do experience this curious "Indian Summer", and to retire them automatically at sixty is one of the profoundest absurdities of the age. Unemployment notwithstanding, no nation can afford to waste energy and ability, especially when allied with experience.

It has often been said that "life begins at forty", but that, too, is poppycock. Life begins to get very difficult at forty for most women, what with the menopause, problem teenage children or cantankerous elderly dependants. But by the mid-fifty's, with any luck, the worst is past. My own menopause had ended abruptly at forty-three, with my sojourn in the hospital, and after that I never looked back.

As 1983 dawned, I was eager for more activity, and although I never set foot outside the United Kingdom that year in some respects it was to be the best and most eventful yet, fulfilling at least one long-standing ambition.

One summer day, a story landed on my desk about a woman of sixty-one who had made a charity parachute jump. When I phoned to ask her how she had felt just before her exit from the plane, she replied, "Funnily enough, I felt strangely calm." That decided me. For long enough, I had been planning a feature on parachuting, something I had always wanted to experience, and now I felt I could not put it off any longer. In consultation with my Bridlington office colleagues, I arranged to take the one-day course at the Grindale skysports centre. As I was over forty-five I had to get my doctor to sign the application form, but that was no problem; he had not seen me in years and had no intention of spoiling the record now!

I was by far the oldest "student" on that particular course, and I must say I enjoyed every minute of it, even though I wrenched my ankle while trying to throw myself sideways on to the grass in a landing practice. There were many humorous moments, including the one when a young fellow's kidney donor card fell out of his pocket, and we debated, with macabre relish, how much good those organs would be to anyone in the unlikely event of his parachute failing to open.

The instruction was first-class, though I did feel, in retrospect, that a film or cartoon sequence would have been helpful in showing us how to make our exit from the plane, as this was something that could not be effectively simulated on the ground. Nevertheless, an incredible amount of information and training was crammed into those obligatory eight hours. We learned the structure and function of our Double-L sports canopy and how to steer in the direction of the target area, how to cope with malfunctions such as a "streamer", a "hang-up" when the tie fails to break and one is left dangling on the line, or a "tail-strike" when the canopy becomes entangled in the rear of the plane and we had to release the Capewell clips fastening the chute to the harness and use our reserve to get down. We were told what to do if we came down in a tree or on a roof, or drifted close to power cables. Again and again we went through the drill of deploying our reserve canopies in the event of the main one malfunctioning.

Nothing was left to chance, and by the end of the day I think we all felt that we could with confidence have joined any crack parachute regiment. By 5 p.m. we were tired but keyed up and anxious to get on with the jump. The wind, however, had freshened, and was too strong for our inexperienced little party. It was, in fact, eight nail-biting days before a space in my diary coincided with suitable dropping conditions, and I found myself once more at Grindale, this time kitted out in borrowed boots and helmets, ill-fitting overalls and, of course, the double parachute pack, the static-line job at the back and the reserve at the front.

My photographer colleague, Ray Brunning, who had been wonderfully supportive, had his camera at the ready, and I knew that, if only for his sake, I could not back out now. Not that I wanted to. I

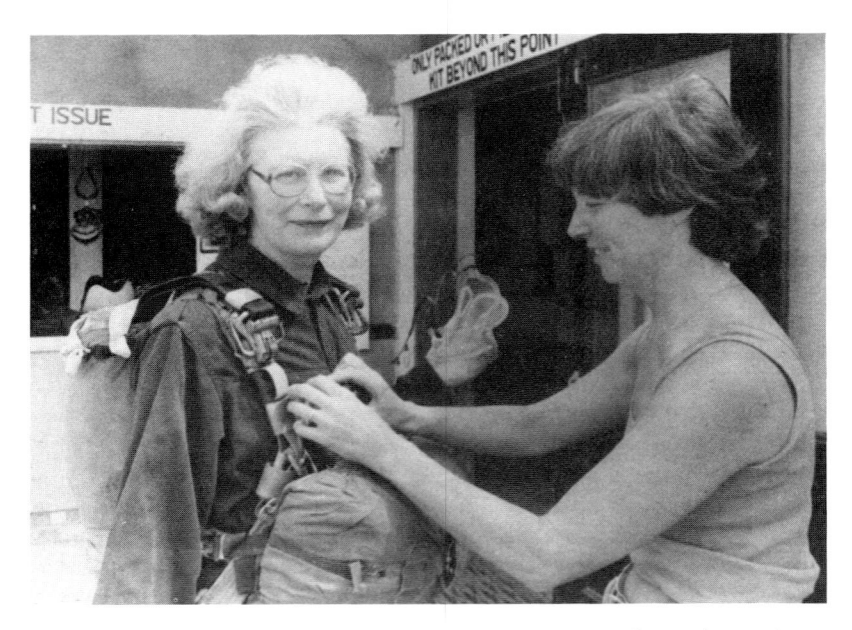

Preparing to jump.

It really worked!

was excited but not scared. The thing I wanted to do most in the world just then was to make that jump.

Four of us at a time were marched to the little Cessna, which had no door and no seats. Having been given our numbers, we were one by one attached by our lines to a strong metal bar in the plane. We sat on the floor, packed like sardines, with our backs to the pilot. The plane took off, and seemed to take a long time to get to the right height as we waited for our numbers to be called.

"Number two — in the door!" I heard the instructor's shouted command at last above the roar of the engine. I shuffled forward and positioned myself as I had been taught, head up, looking at the back of the pilot, feet dangling over 2,000 feet of daylight, hands ready to push myself clear. "GO!" came the order.

I went — but it did not go quite according to plan. One is supposed to assume a stable position, facing earthwards, arms and legs spread wide, as one times the count: "Thousand One — thousand two — thousand three — thousand four," before looking up to check that the canopy has opened correctly. However, I had not quite got the hang of it from the ground practice, so I turned over a couple of times in the air before finding the right position, while the sudden tightening of the harness took my breath away and stifled the carefully-rehearsed count.

However, as I looked up, I could see that the orange and buff canopy had opened, a lovely, reassuring sight, and I was floating gently to earth. I reached up, grasped the wooden toggles and began steering. Gosh — it really worked! Just below, and to the side, I could see No 1, an experienced girl skydiver, also safely on her way down.

As I turned the parachute round through 180 degrees, viewing the horizon and the landscape below, I can honestly say that this was one experience that really came up to expectations, and went way beyond. Of course, there was just the little matter of the landing to come, but I was not unduly worried, and as I reached what I judged to be the obligatory 200 feet from the ground, I turned into the wind and braced my feet and knees together, tucked in my elbows and prepared for the jolt.

I was quite close to the target, but to my annoyance I had landed on the edge of the cornfield, with my lines draped over the low hedge separating it from the airfield. The corn-stalks had broken my fall beautifully, but I felt a bit of an idiot as I tried to disentangle the lines from the hedge and rescue the canopy. Help was at hand, however, in the form of another girl club-member who helped me to free the apparatus and "field-pack" it neatly enough to enable it to be carried back to the packing-shed, where I discovered that even beginners were expected to take their turn at re-folding the equipment under supervision. Ever since then, I have always referred to strong rubber bands as "bunjies".

Despite my first-time mistakes, Ray had taken some excellent pictures of my descent, and these vividly illustrated the article, which caused a bit of a furore, both in and out of the office. This surprised me, as I had thought that sports parachuting had become too commonplace to excite all that much comment. One reader even sent me a bouquet!

I had not attempted to get any sponsorship for this jump, as I was not sure whether I was going to be able to complete the course successfully. The plan was to use the article, if it materialised, to introduce a sponsored jump for a charity. I chose the Save the Children Fund as the most suitable, as I had for many years been a supporter of the organisation, which I felt to be the best in the world. With the help of the local branch, I was moderately successful in securing sponsors — though one doctor (not mine) telephoned to offer £5 if I agreed to call off the second jump! There had been a spate of accidents that summer among charity skydivers, and sports parachuting had taken quite a knock as a result. I think I can say that my couple of enthusiastic and reassuring articles did the sport, as well as the various charities, a bit of good!

The second jump, however, was not quite so pleasurable as the first. Again, I had to wait all day for the wind to drop, and everyone had by that time become a little tired and edgy. My borrowed equipment was particularly uncomfortable and my goggles steamed up so that I could not see very well, with the result that I did not turn in the right direction for the landing. My exit, however, was much better this time; I had realised that one needed to keep one's head right back and follow one's feet down. Although I came down in a ploughed field, once again landing softly and completely unhurt, I felt I had done quite well in the fresh breeze, remembering the drill and reaching out to pull on the lines and deflate the canopy to prevent it from dragging me along the ground. Apparently, however, it was considered a bad slip-up to land with the wind behind you.

I would have very much liked to do some more jumps, but the sport is fairly expensive, in time as well as money, and one would need to feel an encouraging sense of cameraderie if one were to gain real pleasure from it. Somehow, I did not feel that I fitted in all that well at the club, despite the excellent publicity I had given it, so, reluctantly, I decided not to do any more parachuting — for the time being, at any rate, though it seemed a pity. I may not have been all that quick on the uptake, but surely that absence of fear just had to be an asset? I cannot account for it; I am not really a brave person, and it was certainly not a death-wish. I was enjoying life more than ever before.

My project, however, had raised a useful £285 for the Save the Children Fund and provided a couple of "different" articles for the feature, aimed at the younger readers and contrasting with those routine but very necessary parochial paragraphs. In those days it was recognised that the great strength of a local newspaper lay in its systematic coverage of the organised life of the area, something which no other news medium can do half so effectively.

THAT "MOST DISTRESSFUL COUNTRY"

From this point, it was only a step to the next idea — that of "following the money through" to see how it was being used by the Save the Children Fund in the relief of suffering among children everywhere. I would go to the scene of some project somewhere in the world and bring back a first-hand account of how the cash raised by supporters in this country was being spent.

From the Fund's London headquarters I received a batch of literature describing various programmes and decided, as a kind of pilot scheme, to concentrate on the one in Northern Ireland. This had much to recommend it. It could be arranged fairly quickly and inexpensively, to follow on the parachute story, as there would be no need for visas, injections and other complicated preparations. It would also highlight an aspect of the charity's work which is often overlooked — the fact that it operates not only in faraway Third World countries but also right here in the problem areas of the United Kingdom.

Far from receiving any back-up from my newspaper, I was actually told that this project was "too dangerous", and they would not be responsible for my safety. If I went, I would have to go in a freelance capacity!

As I packed my bag on the evening of September 25, 1983, I was listening to the radio. The biggest jail-break in British prison history had just taken place; thirty-eight of the most desperate criminals in the land had escaped from the Maze Prison. This, of course, only added to the topicality of my self-imposed assignment. Early next morning, my well-worn little green Polo was bearing me down the M62 to Leeds-Bradford airport, en route for Belfast.

At the airport, security was naturally tight. Every piece of luggage was meticulously examined and every passenger frisked by very polite, almost apologetic staff. Finally we were allowed on to the plane. At Aldergrove, there was a tense, rather disorganised atmosphere. A tannoy message brought the information that Mrs Dorothy Day, the Fund's Regional Director of Child Care for Northern Ireland, would not be able to pick me up. She could not get through because of the road blocks. I would have to find my own way.

I boarded the airport bus along with other passengers, most of them, I judged, young servicemen in civvies returning from leave. We had not gone far when we were stopped, boarded and checked by worried-looking armed police in flak-jackets. The drive seemed long and slow. When we reached the outskirts of Belfast, the bus slowed to a crawl, and finally became completely locked into the vast traffic-jam caused by the emergency situation.

The driver turned to us: "If yez in a hurry, yez best get out and walk", he said. It seemed good Irish logic, so we did...and I found myself completely lost in that notoriously violent city with more than a score of convicted terrorists on the loose (some had been picked up overnight) and the whole of the security forces out looking for them.

It was then that I made my first major discovery about the people of Northern Ireland. They are the most charming, gentle, helpful folk you could wish to meet! Fifteen years of shooting, killing, bombs and mayhem have not soured your ordinary man and woman in the street or silenced their easy, articulate flow of words. As I said earlier, ours is *not* a violent society. I was passed from one to another until I was put on the right bus to Lisburn Road, and during the short journey the woman in the next seat regaled me with a frank and colourful account of her life story amid the "troubles".

The staff at Popper House, the Save the Children Fund's Belfast headquarters, were up to their necks in work, but made me very welcome, and over the next four days, Dorothy Day and I seemed to forge the same kind of links of mutual regard and friendship that Dorothy Clegg and I had done on our tour of Israel. We had many discussions on the nature of child care in general and the very special problems of Ulster, and I learned a great deal about the situation that had never come through the numerous media reports and documentaries we had all absorbed over the years.

The inexorable way in which normal, decent young people can be drawn into paramilitary factions under "he that is not with us is against us" pressure is something we find difficult to comprehend on this side of the Irish Sea, where both religion and politics are mostly optional things we can take or leave.

In a canteen run by the Quakers on the campus of Long Kesh (the Maze Prison) I talked to the wives of "lifers" — men convicted of serious crimes and deeply involved in sectarian and terrorist killings

— and found them to be intelligent, caring women, agonisingly concerned about the welfare of their men inside and of their growing son and daughters outside. They were a far cry from the kind of thick, mulish, inadequate personalities one usually associated with the hardened criminals.

The same could be said of the people I met and talked to at the SCF's canteen and play-centre next to the curious, classical-styled peach-coloured courthouse in the Crumlin Road, where the "Supergrass" trials were taking place at the time. These men and women, many of whom had come long distances from the country to stand by their kin in their time of betrayal and peril, looked so ordinary, so human; and their gratitude at finding somewhere to sit, have a cup of tea and a snack and use a clean toilet, or where their children could play under skilled supervision, was a tribute to the work of these aid societies.

In some ways, the lot of the families is harder than that of the prisoners, who often have access to recreational, educational and craft materials and facilities which are far beyond the means of their relatives living on social security.

With one of the Fund's workers, a young, beautiful, dedicated woman with the face and gentle manner of a Sister of Charity, though she belonged to no religious order, I toured some of the worst areas of the city — the notorious Divis Flats, the Falls Road, Ballymurphy and White Rock, taking pictures of the empty, barricaded streets, the burned-out cars, the defiant graffiti on the walls — some of it telling the story of the Great Escape — and the strangely artistic murals which, I was told, virtually appear overnight on walls and gable-ends — a terrible waste of talent which in happier times could so much enrich the scene.

Often, over a scene of devastation, I would look up and see the blue-green hills under a soft, autumn sky, a further pregnant reminder of what a lovely country this is, and what tragedy lies in these needless conflicts among her people. I remarked that the housing in some of the Protestant areas appeared to be older and shabbier than that in the Catholic streets, where tremendous efforts seemed to have been made to provide adequate accommodation for the families, but I was told that this was nothing to go by. What really counted was whether you felt secure, accepted, equal before the law and in society.

The beauty of the country was further brought home to me when

The artistic murals which appear overnight.

Some of the worst areas of Belfast.

The defiant graffiti.

I drove with other SCF workers up the Antrim coast to Ballycastle, from where you can look across the shining waters to the Mull of Kintyre. Here, we called at Ramoan, an Intermediate Treatment Centre run with the Fund's support for young offenders in an old vicarage set in fine, rural surroundings.

I heard the staff telling of their successes in bringing Catholic and Protestant boys together, and one story stuck in my mind. One day, one of the workers heard the ominous sound of an IRA rebel song coming from one of the rooms, and hurried in, prepared to quell any possible trouble from the Protestant lads. To his surprise, he found that they had actually asked the Catholic boys to teach them the song — they liked the tune!

As I talked to the boys at work on their various training projects, indoors and out, I noticed once more their musical voices, their easy way with words, so different from the troglodyte grunts which so often pass for speech among young Britons today.

Thanks to Dorothy and her staff, I was able to visit several play-schemes and family welfare centres, see a new play-bus under construction and talk to volunteers who were being trained to operate it. I went to a children's farm where youngsters could spend a peaceful weekend growing things, tending the animals and having fun, and sat in on a conference of probation officers and social workers at which one of the most cheerful aspects was the way in which a number of them challenged the dreary statistics which seemed to indicate that no progress at all was being made in reducing the number of children and young people in trouble. Several speakers told heart-warming success stories from their individual case-loads which argued that the figures were not telling the whole truth.

Between these visits and discussions, I had opportunities to walk around Belfast, wondering again at the calm attitude of these people under their long ordeal of stress, their friendliness and readiness to engage in conversation in shops or cafes. One soon became accustomed to the perfunctory handbag checks at the barriers and the sight of armed police and constant military movement in the street. Yet the danger was always there, just below the surface, and I was told by a Catholic lawyer and his wife who kindly entertained me one evening that few families in the Province had remained untouched by the violence of these past years.

To the end, in fact, I was reminded of this strange blend of charm and latent terror that is Belfast. The taxi-driver who called to take me to the airport bus-stop advised me to let him drive me to Aldergrove itself by a circuitous route, as the city traffic was once more halted by a bomb-alert and he feared I might miss my plane.

Back home, I worked almost round the clock over the weekend to produce a series of articles before the topicality of the jail-break story cooled. Despite their earlier qualms, the newspaper ran them, using my own pictures as illustrations, and as a result of this I was asked to give a number of talks to interested groups. Although I had not taken any slides this time, my inexpensive little camera had done me proud in black and white, and the pictures made graphic back-up material.

Already, a more ambitious scheme to help the Save the Children Fund was taking shape in my mind, but there was only a little of 1983 left, so that would have to wait.

The barriers in Belfast.

A WORLD BENEATH OUR FEET

Seeking an "adventure" to follow the parachute feature, I recalled a remark made by one of the sky-divers I had met, to the effect that nothing would induce him to venture underground. That was it — potholing! So I set about trying to find a caving contact who would be sporting enough to give me a taste of speleology. My luck was in: shortly afterwards I was asked to cover a lecture on caving by Dr Richard Halliwell, of Hull University, and when I spoke to him after the talk, he readily agreed to my request. Some time later, I received an invitation to accompany Richard, his wife, Pat, and other members of the Craven Potholing Club, one of the most prestigious in the country, on a decent of Calf Holes and Browgill Cave, near Horton-in-Ribblesdale in the beautiful Three Peaks area.

As I dressed on the appointed morning, I thought of a comic rhyme I had once seen:

> If you really must climb the Himalayas,
> In spite of dear Grandmother's prayers,
> It is well to begin with wool next to the skin
> And then layers — and layers — and layers!

Not only wool, but a variety of man-made fibres prepared me to fight the cold as I donned my usual underwear, then a set of thermals, then my old gardening trousers, a thin sweater and a thick one, my dog-walking jacket whose torn lining later won approval from the cavers as being supremely suitable for the job, a headscarf and a pair of Moonwalker boots. I also packed a complete change of clothing into a holdall, made arrangements for the dogs to be let out during the day, and set off in the general direction of Bradford, then northwards to Settle and the magnificent scenery of James Herriot's Yorkshire.

Although it was early November, I enjoyed the drive, and arrived at the cottage headquarters of the club in time to see some of the preparations being made by the potholers for future, and more ambitious, excursions, including the construction of the light but immensely strong roll-up ladders they use for the big drops, and the packing and securing of photographic equipment to protect it from the damp and clinging mud. Finally, we were ready for the caves.

To my already bulky gear were added a stout cover-all, kneepads, a pair of rubber gloves, a miner's helmet with lamp, and a big cell battery slung from the waist. This latter piece of equipment was not entirely unfamiliar, as I had already done a feature on coal-mining at Hatfield some years before, and had vivid memories of travelling on the Paddy-train, crawling along the coal-face on hands and knees, and "riding the belt" back to the shaft, so I knew that whatever happened I was not likely to suffer from claustrophobia below ground.

Potholing, however, proved to be the toughest task I had tackled yet, far more arduous, and, I think in retrospect, more hazardous than parachuting. How I emerged from those caves with no broken bones I shall never know!

I almost fell at the first fence — a huge, natural "stile" consisting of wet, slippery boulders. I scrambled clumsily over it and stumbled after the others towards the edge of Calf Holes, where I could hear the crash of a waterfall far below. Here, I discovered that I was going to have to descend by one of those slender ladders I had seen being made, with rungs no thicker than a Churchill cigar. The idea is that you put your toe on one rung, then brace your knee against the rock to make the ladder hang freely while your foot gropes for the next rung, but in my hefty boots I found this difficult, and my arms took most of the weight, aching almost unbearably before I was halfway down. I was attached to the top by a safety rope with a locking device, but all the same I was afraid to let go for fear of a sudden jerk and possible cracked ribs, and, to make matters worse, the darned ladder started swinging round.

The roar of the waterfall sounded nearer and nearer, and at last I heard a reassuring voice: "You're nearly there!" Thankfully, I stepped into about two feet of ice-cold spring water, which came over the tops of my boots, but I was so glad to have my feet on something more or less solid again that I didn't feel the chill.

We set off along the 800-foot passage, stooping at first, then on hands and knees, and finally dragging ourselves along with our noses only a couple of inches above the red-brown water.

But oh, the wonder of those rock formations, picked out in the slender beams from our lamps! I had, of course, seen stalactites and stalagmites in tourist caves before, and on innumerable pictures and films, but these little "shelves" of natural minutiae formed by millions of years of interaction of stone and water were something else! Clusters of tiny spiral helictites stretching back into the rock resembled fairy kingdoms, Liliputian cities or inter-galactic civilisations of another dimension. My hands stretched out instinctively to touch them, but I was warned off: now that caving has become so popular, these formations, like wild flowers and butterflies, are an endangered species.

We emerged from the long crawl into a fair-sized cavern with a 30-foot waterfall, and after a few minutes' respite, I was deputed to lead the party back to the entrance! I managed it, however — but little did I know that we had completed only the easiest part of the venture. Ahead lay Browgill Cave, which, though it is described in the official guide-book as being "suitable for novices, with a little of everything", had, I later discovered, taxed the stamina of even quite experienced cavers.

It began with a walk along a boulder-stream, where one had to feel carefully in the murky waters before putting each foot down. I am afraid I chickened out and crept along the side of the passage, steadying myself by grasping at hand-holds in the rocks.

In some ways, potholing can be like rock-climbing in the pitch darkness, but, as we began to ascend the great slabs and jagged walls that lay in our path, I gradually began to acquire the first glimmerings of caving technique, directing my beam of light on the hazard before me, seeking hand and foot holds, and, as I made use of these, planning ahead like a game of chess.

We reached a part of the cave known as Hainsworth's Passage, into which I was inserted by Richard and his friends. Had I been wearing a bikini, and well greased into the bargain, I might have slipped through without too much difficulty, but resembling as I did a Michelin tyre advertisement, it was not so easy. "I'm stuck - I'm stuck!" I wailed again and again. "Nonsense", would come the reply, "Go to the right a bit". I wriggled desperately, gained an inch here and another there, and eventually hauled myself through, much relieved.

"Let's go through the Hole in the Floor and put Barbara through the Letterbox", I heard next. This really was tough, but I dared not complain again. I managed to get one foot against something solid and pushed and pushed. As shoulders followed head and the rest of

Light at the end of the tunnel!

me began to emerge from the narrow, roughly rectangular slot, I realised that there was a five-foot drop on the other side. "I'm going to fall on my head!" I yelled. The fellows let me sweat for a few moments before making a soft landing for me; then one showed how it should be done, executing a "wheelbarrow" manoeuvre which defies description.

Then came a so-called "staircase", which was really more like a Victorian chimney, minus soot, but minus, also, the footholds into which young Tom might have put his bare toes. Suspended there in the darkness with a rope around my waist, I was grateful for Richard's help as he guided my feet into the unseen crevices in the rock. I had to finish the descent on my own, however, to the accompaniment of much snorting and groaning and cries of "Hey-up — I've lost me welly!"

There were times in that cave when I really felt like giving up. There were huge-looking chasms to be crossed in a stride, menacing shadows creating illusions of height and depth that were quite terrifying, and, in one part, we had to shuffle sideways along a narrow ledge like actors in a Hollywood adventure film, while I prayed not to be the one who falls shrieking into the abyss — which may have been only a foot or two deep but looked bottomless in the gloom.

"The light at the end of the tunnel" was no cliche by the time it came. Tension subsiding, I watched it grow larger and larger, and eventually we were out in the blue and green Dales again, where Pat and some of the others were waiting for us. By themselves, the cavers could have covered the 2,800 feet almost as quickly as they could have walked over the surface, but with me in tow it had taken three hours.

I sank down on a wet, mossy rock, to hear some congratulatory remarks from the other members of our little expedition, including photographer Steve Pickersgill, who had, it turned out, taken come amusing shots of some of my predicaments.

"You will make it clear when you write your piece that no one should ever try potholing unless accompanied by an experienced caver, won't you?" said Richard anxiously. "Don't worry!" I replied, pouring water from my wellies, "By the time I've finished describing the terrors of caving, you are going to have difficulty in recruiting new members."

No fear of that, however, thank God. The spirit of adventure will never die, and like Everest, the caves will always present a challenge, "just because they're there". Even I was back again the following August Bank Holiday to be winched down Gaping Gill, the largest natural chamber in Britain, and to accompany Richard and some of the others through part of the labyrinth of passages which, it has now been discovered, link up with Ingleborough Caves.

Again, it was sad that I had discovered too late a physical and adventurious pursuit that I really liked, and in which I think I would have found congenial companionship. And it was doubly ironic that I should have found the strength and confidence to sample it only when I was coming up to my 60th birthday, whereas in my anaemic, exhausted, periodically pain-racked teens and early twenties, it would have been out of the question.

Nevertheless, my brief excursions beneath moors and fells have had one on-going effect; every time I see those wonderful films shot by that pint-sized genius, Sid Perou — and I think if I could take one video to a desert island it would have to be his "Speleogenesis", in which there is not one human voice or figure, just the stones and the swirling subterranean rivers, the wee creatures of the caves, the droplets and the curtains of sparkling water — I can feel again the clean, cold texture of the rocks under my fingers and the chill of the stream biting through my boots, and smell the strangely attractive dankness of the caverns.

"OPERATION DHAKA"

During 1984, activities centred largely on speaking engagements, which turned out to be a good thing, as it happened. I now had quite a fund of experience to relate, and there was a big demand for anyone with the gift of the gab, their own projection gear and a willingness to turn out in the evenings, particularly in the more remote country districts. My earlier experience as a theatre critic, and the hints that I had picked up by listening to adjudicators at drama festivals also stood me in excellent stead, for, as anyone with any experience of such things knows, travel talks and slide shows can be deadly boring. If, however, the slides are assembled in sequence, so that they tell a story, preferably one which builds up to a dramatic climax, and if the commentary is crisp, and is delivered clearly and with feeling and panache, the result can be extremely effective.

Princess Anne — now the Princess Royal — as President of the Save the Children Fund, had just launched "Operation Dhaka", challenging the National Union of Townswomen's Guilds to raise three-quarters of a million pounds to build a new Child Nutrition Unit to replace the huddle of old, rented buildings in which SCF workers had, miraculously, already brought into being a world-famous medical unit in the Bangladesh capital. As Her Royal Highness is also Patron of the NUTG, it was, in fact, as neat a piece of Pooh-Bah-ism as any of the pen of W.S. Gilbert could have conceived!

As individual Townswomen's Guild Press officers began sending in their reports of coffee mornings, concerts, "fayres" and other events being run to provide money for the appeal, however, it became obvious from the vague, and often inaccurate descriptions, that many of the women who were working so hard to raise the cash had little idea of what it was really for. What was needed, it seemed to me, was for someone to go out there as an impartial, lay observer, unconnected with either the TG movement or the Fund, and bring back, in words and pictures, as full and vivid an account as possible of what "Operation Dhaka" was all about. This would also provide the perfect tie-up between the "parochial" part of my work and the larger issues of social justice on a world scale.

Townswomen's Guild contacts made enthusiastic noises when I suggested the idea, so I approached the SCF with confidence. By any standards, the Northern Ireland project had been a success, resulting in some excellent publicity for the Fund's work. The parachuting lark had not in itself raised a large sum of money but it had certainly "encouraged the others". The articles had been followed by a spate of local stories about individual and group charity jumps, several of them for the same cause — and this in a year when the sport had been badly hit by adverse media coverage. And it didn't stop there: one local councillor who raised a four-figure sum for charity through an arduous sponsored walk, told me later that it had been my example that sparked him off — he did not think he could manage to jump out of a plane but he could at least walk!

It was a surprise, therefore, to find the Fund's Press Office was not, at first, very keen on the idea, and I had to use quite a bit of persuasion to get them to co-operate. At last, however, they agreed that if I managed to get the Soroptimists to help in the planning of the venture, and maybe involved the YWCA as well, their Bangladesh staff would work out a programme of visits to the Child Nutrition Unit and other projects for me.

I contacted the President of the Soroptimist International of Dhaka, lawyer Zebunnessa Rahman, who readily agreed to help, along with other members. The YWCA hostel was closed for refurbishing at the time, so they would not be able to put me up, but Zebunnessa got together with SCF Field Director Alex Gray and it was agreed that I should stay at the Fund's two-bedroomed flat over the administrative headquarters in the Dhanmondi district of Dhaka. This, as it worked out, was an excellent arrangement, as it not only meant that the room was rented for the fortnight, but it also enabled me to appreciate the efficient but no-frills conditions under which the organisation operated.

Getting a visa was not too easy, as journalists are about as popular with Third World governments as they are with motor insurance companies, but, backed by a letter from the SCF area organiser, I finally received one. Then came weeks of boning up on Bangladesh's short but turbulent history as an independent State, and its vexed economic problems, trying to sort out the truth from the chunks of anti-colonialist Marxist propaganda that all too often pass for history today — and getting advice on what to take with me.

I had asked the SCF whether there was some small-sized but useful piece of equipment that they would like me to take out in my hand-luggage, and they sent a list including an otoscope, some disposable hypodermics, and some packets of wooden tongue-depressors which were unobtainable out there. I wrote to Keelers, the London medical instrument makers, for the otoscope, asking whether they could allow some discount as it was for the Save the Children Fund; to my delight, they sent me the £50-plus instrument free of charge. A Hull supplier of surgical necessities was also helpful in getting me a large box of syringes and the tongue depressors. And I was recommended by a Soroptimist who had once worked in Bangladesh to take Rowntree's fruit gums and pastilles and plenty of Smarties for handout sweets, as these survived the climate well.

The Hull YWCA asked me to take out a £20 cheque and some T-shirts and badges as a goodwill gift to their sisters in Dhaka, and by the time I had added a few small gifts, mainly souvenirs with a local flavour for my Soroptimist supporters, there was not much room left for clothes, but that did not matter, as this was not going to be a holiday trip by any manner of means.

By the time I had parked the dogs in the kennels and set off for Heathrow in February 1985, I had left the newspaper job, so my local print outlet was gone. However, this would leave me free to explore alternative, and possibly more influential, media. Moreover, I had discovered that the finest way to get a message over these days is by the spoken word.

The shock TV reports on the African famine, put out at peak viewing times, did, of course, trigger incredible mass-reaction, leading to the huge, multi-million-pound pop events masterminded by Bob Geldof, but the organisers themselves admit that one cannot operate at that pitch all the time. My experience leads me to the firm belief that there is no substitute for constant personal contacts by speakers doing the rounds of the innumerable clubs, classes and societies which proliferate in British communities today. Humping a car-load of equipment, plus a mini-exhibition of products, craft work and aid-society literature night after night to village institutes and church halls, schools and community centres, sometimes braving bad weather and finding only a handful of people there at the end of it, may certainly seem like doing it the hard way, but those audiences are among the most appreciative and attentive one can find.

They have bothered to turn out to hear you and see you, and providing you give them a good show, they will respond. They are not the box-watchers, and it is well worth taking some trouble to reach out to them. They are the kind who get things done, and often they miss out on key TV documentaries and newscasts just because they are so active. And when the hall is full and you know that you are going across well and your audience is with you, it is a wonderful feeling. You can also be sure that if you make the right impression, your show will be talked about in homes, pubs, offices and other gathering-places for weeks afterwards, so your real audience is not limited to the people actually attending the meeting.

The flight to Dhaka was long but pleasant. We came down at Doha in a blazing Arabian dawn to take on a breakfast of delicious aromatic bread and spicy accompaniments, then flew the long haul to Calcutta, a grim-looking airport full of armed guards, where we were allowed to stretch our legs briefly before being hurried back on to the plane for Zia Airport where we landed some 20 minutes later.

I was a little worried about taking my strange hand-luggage through the Customs. What would they make of the syringes and otoscope? Would they think I was in the drugs business? But when I explained that the boxes were gifts for the Save the Children Fund, they smiled and waved me on. At the passport checkout, however, it was not such plain sailing: I was a journalist? What newspaper did I work for? No paper in particular — I was a freelance. But what papers did I freelance for? That was a difficult one, for as yet I had made no regular contacts. Then the Voice of Experience came from behind me in the queue: "Tell him you work for the *Daily Mail* or we'll be here all night!" I did, and it worked. Sorry, Lord Rothermere, but it was only a white lie; I did once work for the Northcliffe Group!

It was a wonderful relief when I saw outside in the waiting crowd a group of the most exquisitely lovely women wearing brightly-coloured saris and holding Soroptimist brochures. They took charge of everything, and soon I was having my first cup of Bangladeshi tea from the northern district of Sylhet — not the best tea in the world, as the country is too flat to provide the right conditions, but most refreshing and drinkable — and meeting the staff at the

Save the Children Fund headquarters.

I soon discovered that European workers are few and far between in Third World projects these days. Apart from Alex Gray and one visiting British doctor, all the trained staff were nationals of the country, and most of the Europeans I met in the next fifteen days were there to learn and observe rather than to teach or to run things.

I made the acquaintance of Panu, who looked after the flat and did the cooking. A magnificent figure, with his fine, white-bearded Bengali face, Panu was a genius at making tempting meals out of simple ingredients. "Prawn curry like?" he would ask, and, on receiving my affirmative, he would produce a delicious concoction, accompanied by small dishes of salads and savouries, including slices of carrot cut into little flower shapes — I have since tried to copy them but my "petals" always snap off. I think Panu liked having the Memsahib to look after for a few days, for he went out of his way to make the table look nice, one day producing a little bird out of mashed potato, which was far too pretty to eat. He also saw to it that the bedroom contained a coil of mosquito-repellant in a saucer, to be lit before one got into bed. There was a net over the bed, but the little beasts seemed to get through it without much difficulty, and I heard their high-pitched whine with dread, as they made a complete meal of every exposed part of me.

My cocktail of typhoid and cholera jabs, polio sugar-lumps and malaria tablets did their work well, and I had no stomach upsets, but nothing really worked against the mosquitoes, which gave me a terrible time, raising huge water-blisters which itched and stung ceaselessly.

Alex and Zebunnessa had between them drawn up a thrilling and far-reaching programme for me. The itinerary compiled by Alex, of course, concentrated on the aid projects which were the focal point of my scheme, but the Soroptimists, all top professional women, had laid on visits and personal hospitality which were to give me a uniquely rounded view of the social and cultural life of the country, and it was this which was to give the resulting "travelling road show" which I took round Britain its breadth, its depth and its colour.

The Bengalis, it seems have always considered themselves to have a distinctive ethnic and cultural entity. The area they occupy in the sub-continent, however, has, over the centuries, known many visitors, and among the most influential were those who brought the faith of Islam to a majority of the people in the area now known as Bangladesh.

During the British presence, Bengal was a part of North-East India, and I was heartened to hear a remark from a mature and highly cultured woman writer (one of the few people I met who had actually lived there at the time) that "When the British were here we had peace and security; we never felt oppressed". When the British left in 1947, that peace was quickly shattered. Unrest broke out between the Muslims and Hindus, and it was decided to partition the country. The States of East and West Pakistan were created, hundreds of miles apart, and united only by the slender thread of a shared religion. It did not work; the people of East Pakistan, with a higher population in a smaller, though more fertile, area, felt themselves to be exploited, given too little political and economic consideration.

As far back as 1952, they won their first cultural victory, defeating a move to make Urdu the official language of the country. The fight to preserve the beautiful and historic Bengali tongue, which derives from ancient Sanskrit, and is written from left to right in 51 elegant characters, cost the lives of a number of protesting students, and they are now remembered annually on February 21, which is designated "language day" and is marked with public readings of Bengali poetry and prose, the singing of patriotic songs and the display of newly published literature.

This was really the start of the revolutionary movement which finally led to the short but terrible war of 1971. From it emerged Bangladesh — desperately poor, but proud and independent, with a Constitution which, according to the copy I was given, is extremely idealistic and ambitious: "It shall be a fundamental responsibility of the State to emancipate the toiling masses, the peasants and workers, and backward sections of the people from all forms of exploitation," it reads. "It shall be a fundamental responsibility of the State to attain, through planned economic growth, a constant increase of productive forces and a steady improvement in the material and cultural standard of living of the people..." And, a page or two later: "The State shall not discriminate against any citizen on grounds only of religion, race, caste, sex or place of birth. Women shall have equal rights with men in all spheres of State and of public life."

Fine words! But making them a reality in a land with so little experience of democratic independence and with so many die-hard customs and economic problems is another matter, and one which is far beyond my ability to summarise here, even if I had the political know-how to comprehend them fully.

There are only three large cities, the capital, Dhaka — the spelling was changed from "Dacca" to try to bring to the Roman alphabet a more accurate idea of the pronunciation, which is slightly aspirated — Khulna, in the south-west, and Chittagong in the east. The rest of the country, a huge, flat plain carved up by the mighty Jamuna River and its tributaries, is dotted with villages and small towns. In the rainy season, it has been said, Bangladesh is not a country with rivers and lakes but a sea with bits of land sticking up out of it!

The Old Town of Dhaka huddles around the river, with its traditional craft. The maze of narrow streets and alleys is choc-a-bloc with brightly decorated rickshaws and other vehicles, and with crowds of people, trading, buying — and, inevitably, begging, displaying a variety of horrible afflictions and deformities to claim our sympathy. We Westerners have to keep reminding ourselves that this has always been very much a part of life here, and that begging is regarded as quite an honourable calling, a disability as a talent to be used.

Spreading out across the line of the old railway track is New Dhaka, miles of wide streets flanked by modern buildings, dominated by the spectacular Parliament complex, which you either love or hate, according to your taste in architecture.

Everywhere, however, the old spills out into the new. There are the ubiquitous tricycle rickshaws — exciting to ride in, and not too uncomfortable if you brace your feet against the footboard, but distinctly hazardous as they weave in and out between cars, buses with passengers hanging on to the outside, brighly painted Bedford trucks, oxen and the occasional flock of goats. There are the street markets, little, open-fronted shops and stalls, some offering freshly-cooked pancake-type eatables — and, of course, the beggars. As a car slows down, a handless stump will be thrust through the open window; as you walk down a street, children stretch out hopeful hands to the international cry of "Baksheesh!" But many do it with a grin, obviously just trying it on every time they spot a European, and we are still rare enough to excite wide, curious stares from young and old alike.

Though the newer part of the town may surprise us at first with its air of sophistication, it is not long before the whiff of an open drain or the sight of a pile of rubbish with pariah dogs, a scabby cat or two, or a consortium of large, dignified black birds rooting about in it, reminds us that this is the Third World. Until you get used to them, the dogs may keep you awake at night with their baying, yelping and fighting, especially if you are an animal-lover. Power cuts, usually of fairly short duration, are not infrequent, and residents usually keep candles at hand. When it happened at the flat, Panu would appear almost instantly at my elbow with one, rather like the Geni of the Lamp.

Nevertheless, the city has a rich cultural life, and efforts are obviously being made to preserve what is best of the past and create a living heritage for future generations. Thanks to my Soroptimist friends, I was able to see a great many examples in my few days with them.

Theatre is very much alive in Dhaka. I was taken by Soroptimist Razia Salam to the Drama Hall — a building which is austere by London West End standards but would no doubt delight the modern school of elemental theatre enthusiasts — to see a fine performance of "Bisarhan" ("Sacrifice") a classic drama by Rabindranoth Tagore, the Shakespeare of Bengali literature. The play, which tells of the twilight of the old, bloodthirsty gods and the dawn of a more humane and rational age, was performed by a team of players who were no less professional and dedicated for having bread-and-butter jobs during the day.

At the home of politician and lecturer Prof. Abu Sayeed Anguri and his beautiful wife, Dilruba, who runs an 87-pupil residential school, I attended a delightful evening of traditional music and dance. Guests sat on big cushions on the floor, dipping their fingers into bowls of spicy food, followed by pinches of herbs wrapped in leaves (for their digestion's sake — the equivalent of our after-dinner mints) while young girls performed age-old story-dances for their pleasure and musicians sang to the beat of drums and the melody of a Bengali harmonium.

The way in which all this is being preserved was explained to me later by Dr Jobeda Khanum, chairman of the Shishu Children's Academy set up in 1976 "to inculcate patriotism, discipline and love for the natural cultural heritage in the entire children's community of the country" — an ambitious project in a land where so many live in primitive rural conditions. But, it is argued, the children of

Bangladesh are no less talented than those of the developed countries:

"Previously, our children did not get much opportunity to develop their talents, but now we are aware of their needs and understand that the children are our wealth," said Dr Khanum. "If we don't save and develop this wealth, in future we shall be bankrupt."

A MESSAGE OF HOPE

This, then, was the background against which the Save the Children Fund was working in Bangladesh, a background not quite so utterly depressing and hopeless as that which I had expected to find. But that made the work seem all the more worth-while — less like banging one's head against a wall or living through a theme from an existentialist play. In winter-time, moreover, the living is just that bit easier for the 85 per cent of the 90-million-plus population who are estimated to live below the poverty-line. It is the dry season. The huge lakes and water-courses which cover so much of the country during the monsoon have receded. Jade-green paddy-fields and other ripening crops stretch across the flat land as far as the eye can see, and the bullock teams are ploughing. There is more work, more food, better communications.

However, a steady stream of worried parents still make their way to the world-famous Child Nutrition Unit operated by the Fund, anxious to find out why their little ones are not thriving. On our arrival, Zebunnessa Rahman and I were greeted by the Medical Director, the beautiful and distinguished Dr Sultana Khanum, who was delighted with the gifts I had brought, and willingly gave me a rundown on the work of the unit and a message of hope and thanks to bring back to the British Townswomen who were working so hard to raise the money for the new building.

Then we were introduced to Dr Q.M. Iqbal Hossain, who took us first to the teaching area. It has been found that ignorance, rather than privation, is the main cause of child malnutrition today, he told us. Mass starvation is not at the moment the big problem in Bangladesh. The land is extremely fertile, new high-yield crops are being introduced, and there should be enough food for everyone. But, despite tightly-knit family and community traditions, repeated disasters, both natural and man-made, have caused a break in the handing down of mother-to-daughter lore, especially in the squalid bustees, to which flood-victims tend to drift when their villages are inundated.

Surprisingly to Western minds, it is the first child which is most at risk. Babies are breast-fed, but lactation does not seem to have the same degree of contraceptive effect that it does in other communities, and soon a second child is on the way. When it arrives, it has first claim on the natural food supply, and the older child, not properly weaned on to solid food, or not given sufficient of it, starts to go downhill. The custom of giving priority to the elderly, so commendable in many ways, also means that sometimes the growing child is given insuffucient for its needs. The first task of the CNU, therefore, is to teach the young mothers how to prepare food from the cheap, easily obtained ingredients available. We saw a huge pot of nourishing, thick broth being prepared from rice, lentils, onions and other fresh vegetables, with a little oil added to give it taste-appeal and extra nutrients. Nearby, mothers were being instructed by their own countrywomen in simple household management and basic home hygiene.

In the out-patient department, we saw children being weighed and examined by paramedics, who pass on the serious cases to the doctors. Immunisation is carried out and family-planning and antenatal advice given and aids dispensed. We were shown one of the simple maternity kits which are issued to expectant mothers. These include, in addition to antiseptics, a small piece of sterilised surgical blade for cutting the cord — it was found that if a whole blade was put in, some of the less co-operative husbands used it for shaving! Some husbands, however, were becoming more understanding about birth control, we were told.

Advanced cases of malnutrition are admitted to the 60-bed intensive care unit, and here Zebunnessa and I saw some heartbreaking cases, though many of the wee patients were well on their way to regaining the seventy-five per cent of normal weight at which point they can be discharged back to their newly-trained mothers: "We know it is working, because we don't get the same ones coming back again," Dr Khanum had told me.

Among the most seriously ill children in this part of the hospital, however, were those suffering from measles, a killer in the Third World. During my stay I met two doctors, one British and the other Bangladeshi, who were collaborating with Dr Khanum in pioneering a new measles vaccine which can be given to babies as young as four months. Bangladesh, with its massive population and equally massive problems, is an ideal place for finding out how best to administer this kind of immunisation on a large scale. A watch is also kept for TB symptoms, and if they are found, the whole family is screened. Home visits are made where necessary and cases followed up — patients are treated as individuals and do not just disappear into the teeming stews of Dhaka to start the cycle of deprivation all over again.

Attached to the CNU are a small but useful laboratory, with a blood-bank, a library and lecture-rooms for the use of the many students and nutrition experts who come from all over the world to this remarkable place. All this means that the premises, most parts of which have that characteristic shabby, well-worn look typical of the tropics, are very cramped and crowded with patients and visitors, not to mention the staff, who number about seventy-five.

Play, however, is very important for children, forming a big part of their rehabilitation after intensive treatment, and a small corridor area is set aside for this purpose, volunteer helpers doing valuable work as play-leaders. One of these, Mrs Sue Baddeley, wife of a British Army officer who was assisting in a training scheme with the Bangladeshi forces, told me of her great pleasure in working with the children, who were particularly fascinated by her blonde hair, and were not above pulling strands of it out to examine it more closely!

While we were talking to Mrs Baddeley, I noticed that there were not many toys for the children to play with, and suggested getting up a fund back home so that we could send a few boxes of playthings out to them. "Forget it!" I was advised. "We would never get them — they would just disappear on the way. It is no use sending gifts through the ordinary mailing system. Just keep sending the money to London HQ."

I did not forget about it, however (remember the story of the organ?) A few days later, I was visiting the Rehabilitation Centre for the Paralysed, just round the corner from the SCF headquarters, where I met one of the most remarkable young women I have ever encountered, the ever-cheerful and enthusiastic founder-project-coordinator, Valerie Taylor. As Valerie showed me round and introduced me to some of her staff — several of them paraplegics — I saw some very attractive craft work being turned out, including big, wooden toys. "How would it be if I left you some money to make some toys for the children in the CNU?" I suggested. Valerie was delighted: "It would give our people something specific to work for and would be nice for the children, too," she said.

I looked in my purse, which seemed to be stuffed with takas, the local currency. On the advice of my Hull Soroptimist friend who runs the Bureau de Change at Thomas Cook's, I had taken my travellers' cheques in American dollars — and in February 1985, the dollar was at an artificial "high", so, while in Bangladesh I felt like a comparatively rich woman. I peeled off a couple of notes with several noughts on them: "Would that make a reasonable batch of toys?" I asked. Valerie smiled: "That would do very nicely," she replied. And some weeks after my return to Britain I heard that most of the cash had been used to make a baby-walker type of trolley which would not only amuse the kids but also help them to strengthen their muscles, and the balance had been spent on creating some nice, big wooden puzzles.

There was, I was pleased to discover, a lot of interaction between charity projects in Bangladesh, and this was no exception. The Save the Children Fund sponsors paralysis victims for treatment at the centre, including the charming receptionist, Mohua Paul, who greeted me on arrival. The paraplegic staff are a great inspiration to the in-coming patients, who often arrive feeling that they will never be useful and active again. Madhab ch. Kangsa Banik, who is tetraplegic, is not only a counsellor and teacher at the centre, but is a well-known artist, for a number of his attractive paintings done with a brush or pen inserted in a splint on his arm, in which he has a little movement, have found their way on to charity greetings cards.

Valerie told me that many of the patients had sustained their injuries in falling from trees, while others had suffered broken necks when heavy loads carried on the head had shifted awkwardly. A wide range of treatments are given at the centre, and some patients are encouraged to run little street stalls to earn a useful taka or two to help them towards independence. I was also told how patients' confidence and self-respect grew as they learned how to cope with day-to-day problems such as incontinence, and how necessity often proved the mother of invention as simple aids were adapted to local needs — like the inexpensive low-level trolleys which paraplegics there find more suitable than wheelchairs in homes where most members of the family sit or lie on the floor rather than using chairs or couches.

Again and again in my journeys in Third World countries, I have discovered how simple and inexpensive things are often much more practical and realistic than costly high-tech gadgets — a lesson which I think medical and welfare authorities in the West could take to heart!

My visit to the Child Nutrition Unit had been brief, but it had made a deep impression, and I had secured some excellent pictures which were to tell the story better than words. In a country like this, with its teeming millions of poor and disadvantaged people, one cannot deal in numbers — one has to focus on one. For me, this was little Masuda, an abandoned baby who had been found starving and close to death and brought into the unit.

The Save the Children Fund claim a ninety-five per cent survival rate for the unit, and I use Masuda's picture as proof that this is not achieved by turning away the worst cases. Masuda — the nurses gave her that name, for she had none when she was brought in — had, in fact, given up the struggle for life, and could no longer take in food by the mouth, so she was having to be fed through a tube in her nose. She lay simply in her cot, a tiny bundle of charcoal-grey skin stretched over stick-like bones, not crying, not caring. In the few minutes I spent in that ward, I saw the nurses repeatedly picking her up, trying to get a few more drops of fluid into her, talking to her — loving her back to life, for babies cannot live without love. Poor mite! I don't know whether she was one of the lucky ninety-five per cent, but her little face, shining out from my screen or looking down from the wall at an exhibition, has moved many hundreds of people and set them rooting in their pockets and fumbling for their chequebooks.

On the day I was to visit and take pictures of the site for the new unit, already purchased with £40,000 of the money collected by the Townswomen's Guilds, I had a piece of good luck. John Sanday, the architect, was visiting Dhaka. It was a chance meeting between Alex and John in Khatmandu, where the latter has his Asian headquarters, which led to the commission, a coincidence which could not have been more fortunate, for John is one of the world's leading authorities on the preservation of historic buildings.

There was already a building on the Dhaka site, but it was by no means historic, just a crumbling relic from the colonial days, and there was no way it could be adapted into a functional hospital unit, so it was scheduled for demolition, together with its tatty outbuildings, and in its place is now rising the two-storey hospital block.

All the fine trees on the site are being preserved to offer a welcoming shade, and the new buildings, while giving staff excellent conditions in which to work, are designed in such a way that they will not constitute a cultural shock for mothers coming from poor districts with their young ones by confronting them with something clinical and unfamiliar. Again, simple design, using local, well-tried materials, are proving not only adequate and workable but actually better than complicated, imported things.

Expansion, however, is not envisaged, Alex told me: "In a country like Bangladesh, if you start expanding, where do you stop?" It is intended that the new Child Nutrition Unit will be a power-house for teaching and learning, so that its work and influence, not its physical size, will do the expanding.

As I stood there in the afternoon sunshine, looking at the plans over John's shoulder, I felt again that curious sense of drama, as though the poor little frightened, anaemic teenager that was once me was looking down at this determined woman who had overcome so many disappointments and setbacks to get to this place at this moment. Here, after all, was the ultimate goal of the whole project; here I was, camera in hand, at the nerve-centre of "Operation Dhaka".

THE RIVER PROJECT

The fund runs another urban relief programme at Khulna, a large town in the south-west, but for contrast Alex invited me to accompany him to what is known as the Jamuna River Project, to see how the workers coped with rural conditions.

As the clumsy Landcruiser, expertly piloted by Alex, bucked and kicked over the rough ground, I was thankful that I had at one time learned to ride a horse! I use the word "piloted" advisedly, for we seemed to be airborne for at least fifty per cent of the time.

We left Dhaka in the early afternoon, travelling more than 100 miles through surprisingly beautiful country, the green-paddy fields stretching on either side of the bumpy track and the kapok tree displaying its full winter glory of scarlet blossoms, soon to be replaced by black pods holding the familiar fluffy cushion-filler. All that was missing were the famous purple water-hyacinths, not yet in bloom.

We passed through dusty little towns, scruffy chickens and pretty, naked toddlers scattering before us. North of Jamalpur we crossed the river by an antiquated but functional ferry, hand-operated by a couple of men pulling on a rope, and I took a quick camera-shot of a crimson sunset over the water.

As darkness fell, tiny points of light began to show from the bamboo dwellings half hidden among trees on the small hillocks which stood above monsoon water level — the only relatively safe places to build. Suddenly, all those tasteless population-explosion jokes about there being "nothing else to do in the evening" made sense. It is no joke. Imagine living with one's family in one room, with just an oil lamp for illumination. There is no radio, no television, probably no reading matter for study or pleasure, no gas, electricity or piped water. And, as one Bangladeshi friend had remarked earlier, with disarming frankness: "Everything in this country is exceptionally fertile, the soil, the animals — and us!"

Alex brought the Landcruiser to a halt at last, and we stepped out into the darkness. The night sky was a breathtaking blaze of stars, but just then I would have traded the whole galaxy for a few street lamps as I stumbled down the sandy track to the Pullakandi headquarters of the SCF River Project, which, I had been told, started as a disaster relief operation in 1974 and had proved so successful that it had been established on a permanent basis.

The staff welcomed us warmly. With the aid of a few Smarties I made friends with two wide-eyed youngsters in the kitchen, and soon we were eating a plain but adequate meal and drinking tea with bay-leaves floating in it, all by the light of a hurricane lamp. I was introduced to the primitive "ablutions block", which, nevertheless, boasted a supply of good, clean, cold water from a tubewell, and to the bamboo hut where I was to spend the next three nights — not without some trepidation as I listened to strange rustlings in the thatch.

Again, the facilities provided for the workers, though healthy and adequate, were simplicity itself. At Pullakandi, for instance, the VIP's were the vaccines, which had their own refrigerator, powered by cylinders of gas. Not a penny is wasted, yet the campus is extraordinarily efficient. There is a clinic, with facilities for immunisation and family planning, a children's centre and school, offices, stores and even a little "conference room", all housed in cool, basic bamboo structures. I think it was those meticulous records of patient-care which I saw at Pullakandi which finally banished from my mind this preconceived impression that rural Bangladesh was just a seething mass of nameless surplus humanity!

There are six villages in the River Project, Pullakandi, Bahadurabad, Katherbil, Borkhal, Kalakanda and Harichandi. The morning I set off with Field Officer Hafiz al-Montazir to visit Bahadurabad, I was offered a bicycle, but I declined, as it was many years since I had ridden one and I was not very good at it even then (another part of my anxiety-ridden youth). So we went on foot, tramping across the seemingly interminable sandy waste of a dried river bed, scored with cart-tracks. On the way, Hafiz pointed out a small groundnuts plantation which the SCF had introduced to provide villagers with a useful crop.

Parts of this area, I found out, were rather like a sort of huge, inland Spurn Point, the monsoon water constantly washing soil from one area and piling it up in another. Recently, the villagers have been allowed to claim "new land" and cultivate it themselves.

A small boy ferried us across a narrow stretch of water in a boat which looked far too big for him to handle, and soon we reached the village, where I was introduced to a smart little class of youngsters who were being taught the Bengali alphabet. Not far away, outside a picturesque creeper-covered building, a group of women were sitting on the ground listening to one of their number who had been trained by SCF to explain family planning to them with the aid of simple diagrams. Several young lads were listening too, and I remembered what I had been told about the gradual breakdown of male prejudice; it seemed promising that these boys were soaking up the idea in a matter-of-fact way at an early age.

Those two "classes" were not unconnected; literacy is the key to unlock the cycle of deprivation. The simple ability to read and write can lead to a better job, which in turn provides a higher standard of living, a chance to provide for one's old age, so that one does not have to depend on one's children. Then, and only then, will birth control really make sense to these people.

"Literacy means independence," Project Manager Zahid Hussain had told me back at the Pullakandi complex. "In the next 10 years we are hoping to raise the literacy rate in this area to 80 per cent."

At Bahadurabad, I watched mothers bringing their wee ones to the clinic, and discovered that the main problem at this particular time was not malnutrition but scabies, a horrible parasite which burrows into the flesh, particularly in the warm, damp areas of the body. These infested babies were a pitiful sight, and the irritation and distress they suffered must have been almost unbearable. But I noticed, not for the first time, how stoical Third World children were, how trusting. There was little crying.

Early next day, Alex and I set off for Katherbil, the northernmost centre, and the poorest, where there was to be a Sports Day. This was a fantastic experience, more than 300 boys and girls taking part in races and other events — including a Bengali version of Musical Chairs, played to the clashing of a pair of cymbals! It was strange, and charming, to see this Victorian parlour game played in up-country Bangladesh, and I have since wondered whether this was one of the nicer things left behind by the British.

Everyone was dressed in their best. A tiny flower-girl in a red sari offered her wares of crimson blossoms, and Alex and I were garlanded with real and articifical blooms. Like Masuda in the intensive care ward, this little lass was destined to raise more money than she did that day by selling her basket of flowers, for her picture is among the most successful in my collection for coaxing donations out of audiences.

The Sports Day arose out of an educational project undertaken by the Fund, whereby it provides extra teaching for primary pupils to give them a better chance of making it to the State secondary schools, and it was great to see so many healthy, happy kids working off surplus energy, just like their European counterparts, but during the lunch-break I was brought up sharply against the grimmer side of things again, for Katherbil, the poorest village of all, has the only feeding-centre which is kept going right through the cool winter months, when conditions are normally easier. Here I captured some of my most poignant pictures of mothers with their tiny, sick infants. One was pitifully trying to feed her baby, but clearly something was wrong, as the child's distended stomach showed the characteristic signs of kwashiorkor.

We left them in the capable hands of the SCF workers and went back to the games. Alex presented the winners with their prizes — nice, useful things such as oil lamps, bowls, plates and water-jugs, which I should have been well pleased to take home to Mum when I was at school.

On the way back, we ran into one of those little incidents which shows how hazardous movement can be in this area. As we were trying to pass one of the large, slow-moving bullock carts, the fragile lip of the narrow, shored-up road crumbled beneath the nearside front wheel of the Landcruiser, which lurched alarmingly sideways.

"Everybody out!" ordered Alex crisply. I needed no second bidding, executing a quick exit-left out of the passenger door and slithering down the steep, sandy bank towards the wet paddy-field below. Fearing that the heavy vehicle might be about to roll on top of me, I scrabbled for a foothold. Brown hands reached down and pulled me clear. Standing, a little shaken, on the road, I realised that I was still clutching the bag containing my camera, and, journalistic instinct overcoming panic, I grabbed a couple of shots. Fortunately, the sturdy Landcruiser did not follow me down the bank. Although the scene had seemed to be deserted seconds before, a crowd quickly collected — people seem to pop up out of the ground in Bangladesh! — and the sheer weight of willing man and boy-power soon had us back on the road.

Back at the flat in Dhaka, I looked in a mirror for the first time in days. Sun-scorched, limp-haired and covered in big, red insect bites,

I looked like a character out of the Japanese prison camp TV serial, *"Tenko"*. But it had been worth it!

PEOPLE AGAINST POVERTY

The Families for Children orphanage in Dhaka has become world-famous following the success of British Airways hostess Pat Kerr in achieving TV documentary coverage for a proposed expansion scheme there. I met Pat at the orphanage, and we discovered that we had a lot in common.

The orphanage, one of several founded in developing countries by a Canadian woman, Sandra Simpson, houses more than 400 children, from babies to teenagers, offering them good educational facilities as well as physical care. A regular stream of young volunteers from other countries help the 100 local ayahs to look after the children, and I met several of them as I went round the place. I also captured a superb picture of one of the young nurses holding a sleeping child, while others, in their birthday suits, peered cautiously round a doorway — it made a perfect Christmas card!

As I walked across the courtyard I was mobbed by the children, who love to see visitors, and who wonderingly fingered my skirt and pulled at my stockings, apparently fascinated by this strange second "skin" which appeared to be new to them.

The building seemed shabby and overcrowded, but it was good to know that, with the support of the powerful airline company, there was shining hope for the future.

In the course of my travels, incidentally, I was glad that my contact had advised me to take tubes of fruit gums and pastilles, for I discovered that, like loaves and fishes, they had quite magical properties! If you offer sweets to a couple of dark-eyed youngsters, you find on turning round that 50 more pairs of eyes are looking at you. Rowntrees never let me down; I could swear that one tube grew longer as I held it out, and there was always another sticky little goody left when one thought one had dispensed the last. A whole "multitude" was fed on one occasion — and there was even one left for Grandma!

What Bangladesh needs most is peace, within and without her borders, coupled with strong, stable, honest government, uniting all people in a common objective, plus massive international aid, trade and co-operation. But instead of crying for these seemingly unattainable moons, there are a number of people who are grasping the nearest bit of dirt, disease, want or ignorance and doing something about it. Oh yes, there is greed and corruption far beyond the comprehension of people like ourselves, who, despite all our moans, don't know we are born in this respect. I did not see it — I wouldn't, would I, given so little time and scope? But, thanks to Alex and Zebunessa and their friends, I did meet many people, and see many enterprises, which offer hope in a cynical world.

Latifa Akanda, for instance, might be described as the Mother Theresa of Dhaka. Mrs. Akanda, who is Associate Professor of Islamic History and Culture at Dhaka University, has to tread a delicate path between Muslim custom and the laws imposed by the secular government in her work of rescuing unwanted babies and finding homes for them. Little more than six months before my visit, Mrs. Akanda had formed a committee of about thirty-five people to help her, and I was, in fact, the first overseas visitor to her tiny "Suromita Child Care and Rehabilitation Centre". Because of the limited funds, it had so far been possible to take only three or four babies at a time, and to keep them for just a short while, placing them before they started to need solid food and more comprehensive care, but it was hoped to expand later.

Razia Salam introduced me to Jahanara Huq and Roushan Jahan, leaders of the "Women for Women" movement. Established in 1974 by a number of educated women, it is a research and study group which aims to create awareness among the policy-planners about the need for improvement in the status of women, and "to mould public opinion in support of women's stand against oppression and exploitation."

Another world-renowned woman to whom I was introduced was Dr. Sultana Zaman, Associate Professor in the Department of Psychology at Dhaka University. Dr. Zaman is doing battle on behalf of Bangladesh's mentally handicapped, and it was she who showed me round "Kalyani" (rough translation, "Welfare") which is giving education and craft training to a number of children and young people.

It was a moving experience when the children gathered to sing traditional and patriotic songs for their visitors, who found it hard to believe that they were handicapped. I cannot stress too strongly the joy and encouragement which these aid projects gain from visits by sympathetic supporters, especially those who have travelled over oceans and continents to meet them. This was the message which came over loud and clear wherever I went.

The work of artist Surayia Rahman has been described as "unique and unforgettable", and I shall certainly not forget my meeting with this charming and gentle woman. Best known for her work with oils, she developed a semi-cubist style and her favourite themes were feminine or religious. But now, this sincere and dedicated artist has accepted another challenge — to develop the Nakshi Kantha Tapestry School and to teach previously untrained and uneducated women to become skilled embroideresses, capable of bringing her intricately patterned visions of folk lore and everyday Bangladeshi scenes to life.

I saw the fruits of this at the Skill Development Centre for Underprivileged Women where lovely wall-hangings were made, and where I was able to buy a smaller piece for 900 takas — about £30 — to bring home to be used to raise funds for "Operation Dhaka". Started by a group of ten women, headed by another Canadian, Maureen Berlin, in 1982, the Skill Centre now employs 200 women, who work full or part-time in big, airy rooms while their babies are cared for in a creche and older children receive lessons.

In complete contrast to the serene Surayia was Aktheri Begum, the strong-minded leader of one of the "Karika" co-operatives run by the Bangladesh Hasta Shilpa Samabaya Federation, established in 1974 to develop, revive and promote the rich crafts of the country, and to provide employment, especially for the women.

Though her home is still in a "bustee", or shanty area — ironically only a few yards from the splendid Sonargaon Hotel in Dhaka, — it already shows signs of a rising standard of living. The walls may be made of rusty corrugated iron and the roof of bits and pieces of wood and scrap metal, but there is a real brick path around it instead of mud, and furniture within, including a cabinet full of china brought home by a son who is working in Saudi Arabia. At the rear of the house, Aktheri grows melons on a vine draped over a trellis. There is a bracelet on her arm and she is able to offer visitors fresh coconut and home-made pickled olives.

For many of Bangladesh's poor, Karika provides a full-time trade, while for others it is a part-time, seasonal occupation, helping to raise their standard of living. Some have been able to buy their shanty homes — and while we Europeans may exclaim "Big deal!" it is at least a start, and frees the occupants from the clutches of greedy landlords.

Aktheri, an efficient and resolute organiser, is a shining example of what the poor can do for themselves with just a little help. She and her husband have brought up five sons and a daughter, and have known the depths of privation and despair. Now, they hold their heads high, and the quality of their lives continues to improve.

Asrukana Das, the National Secretary of the YWCA, had a heartening story to tell of Christian outreach throughout Bangladesh. The YWCA, which runs a 65-bed hostel for working girls in Dhaka, together with kindergartens, schools and adult classes, training schemes and economic development projects, also weighs in with a will whenever there is a flood or other disaster.

In the capital, and at seven branches, hundreds of women and girls are given instruction in the production of beautiful jute craftwork, in tailoring, sewing and embroidery, flower-making, batik printing and the production of confectionery and preserves for sale to local shops. Management skills are taught, and all this can lead to employment in the open labour market and consequent independence. There are health programmes, loan schemes and savings plans — and at Mymensingh there is even a pig-rearing project!

Besides these groups and individuals, Bangladesh's small but growing community of highly-qualified professional women are working through international organisations such as Business and Professional Women's Clubs, the International Federation of University Women, and, of course, my own dear Soroptimist International, to help raise the standards of the less fortunate citizens of their country.

"This is not a defeated country, for all its problems," I wrote when I came back. "The proud Bengali face stares boldly at you from beneath headband or shock of black hair. The children look with a wide-eyed wonder into the future — a future which we can all help to ensure will be better than the past."

THE RELUCTANT EGOTIST

The return journey from Dhaka was exhausting. We were delayed for hours by an electrical fault in the plane, eventually righted, it appeared, with the friendly co-operation of two Dutch technicians from the KLM line.

I arrived home tired but elated, thrilled with the material I had collected in that crowded fortnight. There was an anxious wait for the transparencies to be developed, but when they came through I knew that, notwithstanding my cheap camera and lack of technical know-how, I had another winner.

I got a couple of spots on local radio, sent articles to the Soroptimist and Townswomen's Guild journals, and soon the bookings began coming in, slowly at first, which tried my patience, then with gathering momentum. I was invited to address a big rally of Lakeland Soroptimists and other socially-aware citizens in Penrith. Then came an invitation to give two lectures in the Isle of Wight. Later, I was engaged to share a platform at a big Third World Day in Salisbury with a Cambridge professor of nutrition, where I found to my considerable relief that each of my pictures, amateur though they were, brought to vivid and colourful life the factual statistics he had so expertly given.

Inquiries came from Cheshire, from Tyneside, from Northampton, and from many parts of West and North Yorkshire — Harrogate, Wakefield, Selby, Pontefract — while on my home ground I covered everything from tiny house groups to three-figure audiences in large halls, from UNA meetings and local authority classes to gatherings of women's organisations and church society members, sometimes giving two shows in one day. With sterling help from my friends of the Baha'i community, I put on my own show in the wake of the 1985 cyclone disaster, and set up stands at a number of well-attended public exhibitions on both banks of the Humber.

I have long since lost count of the number of shows I have given, and of the amount of cash collected. The financial benefits are, in fact, hard to assess, because I asked all the Townswomen's Guilds to put their contributions directly into their own "Operation Dhaka" collections. I have actually turned down offers of fees and donations, as I felt that certain organisations were themselves good causes — but I knew that many of the people concerned with these bodies wore several "hats", and I am sure I set many thoughts in the direction of future Third World support.

Direct money-raising, however, was not my main object. My speaking and writing are mainly designed as a voluntary public relations operation — and I must admit that I know of no other quite like it. Apart from anything else, it offers a little "thank-you" to supporters for their past achievements, and we all know how valuable a pat on the back can be in spurring us on to fresh efforts. I feel, too, that the many wonderful charity workers in the country, who do prodigious things to help projects that they will never be able to visit themselves, have a right to the kind of information that someone like myself, as an impartial observer, is able to bring to them.

Of course there were disappointments. For instance, apart from my interviews on local radio, which was very co-operative, I was unable to break through to the commercial media. Something strange, and rather sinister, seems to have happened to the Press in the past few years. Newspapers appear to have polarised. On the one hand, we have the down-market tabloids and, on the other, the up-market "heavies", interested only in big names. Neither provides a market for competently-written articles of general interest, while the women's journals, which at one time were following the trend towards a broader, more intelligent view of women's affairs, seem to have returned to a pre-occupation with fashion, food and repetitious syndicated features on slimming, diet, exercise, soap stars and the like. And despite their initial enthusiasm, the heirarchy of the National Union of Townswomen's Guilds did not respond to my project or promote it as widely as I had expected them to do. But no matter they raised that £750,000 — and more — and, in any event, I had just about as many speaking engagements as I could handle.

There are wonderful moments to look back upon. There were the Bangladeshi exiles who came up to thank me for giving what they described as a sensitive and accurate picture of their country and people. There was the little boy who had never been to his country of ethnic origin, and who sat enthralled throughout the show.

And there was the day when I received special permission to hand in at Buckingham Palace a large album compiled for Princess Anne, containing a full account in words and pictures of everything I had seen on my visit to Bangladesh.

One day, when I was checking the slides before a show, I noticed how informal they were, and it dawned on me that I had seen something no royal or VIP visitor would ever see — the Child Nutrition Unit and other centres on an ordinary working day, without security guards, red carpets, television camera crews or best bibs-and-tuckers. I received a warm and friendly acknowledgement from the Palace, and later I was told that, instead of being stored in the vaults and lost for ever, the album had been passed on to the London headquarters of the Save the Children Fund to be placed in their library for the use of the staff and visitors — a most practical and imaginative gesture on the part of the royal recipient. I like to think that in time to come that book may become a little piece of social history.

Irony pursues me to the last: who would have thought that the precocious brat who found her playmates babyish and boring, or the sex-scared young woman who could not summon up a vestige of maternal instinct, and secretly rather agreed with W.C. Fields that there could not be much wrong with a fellow who hated kids, would end up spending a good part of her time drawing attention to the needs of the world's children?

When I first heard the popular song, *"My Way"*, I thought it propounded a dreadul philosophy. To set one's own petty little goals and then to feel childishly pleased because one had come somewhere near achieving them, went against all the moral principles on which I had been brought up. A man's reach should exceed his grasp, we were told. We should set our sights on some Great Ideal, whether we called it Christ or Jehovah, Mahommed, Baha'u'llah or whatever. Then, at the end of the day, we should be able to turn to that Ideal and say, "I tried to do it *your* way. I fell light-years short, but I tried!"

So, trite as they may be, the words of the song speak to my condition too aptly to escape quotation:

> *I've loved, I've laughed and cried, I've had my fill –*
> *my share of losing.*
> *And now, as tears subside, I find it all so amusing –*

To think I did all that, and may I say, not in a shy way.
Oh no – oh no, not me! I did it my way.

I'll not end there though. My birth got off on the wrong foot. My marriage got off on the wrong foot. My so-called "retirement" certainly got off on the wrong foot. Only one great life-mark remains to be bungled. But I hope I haven't reached that "final curtain" yet by a long way! I am enjoying my Indian Summer too much, and still have hopes of gathering in a greater harvest.

At the height of his career, David Ben Gurion was asked by a schoolgirl, "On what day of your life were you most satisfied?" Thoughtfully, the veteran statesman replied, "If a man is satisfied, what does he do then? A satisfied man no longer yearns, no longer dreams, no longer creates, no longer demands. No, no — I have never had a single moment of satisfaction!"

Neither have I. Come to think of it, I feel just the same as I did when I was 16 — I am still waiting for life to begin...

THE END